THE PENGUIN CLASSICS

EDITED BY E. V. RIEU

L 5

TACITUS
ON BRITAIN
AND GERMANY

A NEW TRANSLATION OF
THE 'AGRICOLA' AND THE 'GERMANIA'
BY H. MATTINGLY

PENGUIN BOOKS

Penguin Books Ltd, Harmondsworth, Middlesex

U.S.A.: Penguin Books Inc., 3300 Clipper Mill Road, Baltimore 11, Md
[Educational Representative:
D. C. Heath & Co., 285 Columbus Avenue, Boston 16, Mass]

CANADA: Penguin Books (Canada) Ltd, 47 Green Street,
Saint Lambert, Montreal, P.Q.

AUSTRALIA: Penguin Books Pty Ltd, 762 Whitehorse Road,
Mitcham, Victoria

SOUTH AFRICA: Penguin Books (S.A.) Pty Ltd, Gibraltar House,
Regents Road, Sea Point, Cape Town

—

First published 1948
Reprinted 1951, 1954

Made and printed in Great Britain by
Richard Clay and Company, Ltd,
Bungay, Suffolk

CONTENTS

INTRODUCTION

THE *Agricola* of Tacitus, the biography of the most famous governor of Roman Britain, is part of our national story, and as such has a direct claim on our interest. The *Germania*, a detailed account of a great people that had already begun to be a European problem in the first century of our era, should still have a message for us in the twentieth. The story of the hero and the story of strange countries that were combined in Homer's *Odyssey* have now, at a later stage of literature, come to receive separate treatment.

It is to the modern British reader, then, that this version is offered. As he is probably unfamiliar with much detail that is necessary for the full understanding of the story, it will be well to say something about the author and his works and the conditions of the age in which he wrote. The early parts of the introduction will be better understood when the whole of it has been read.

The general reader may like to be warned that sections xi–xiv of this Introduction are less immediately necessary to the understanding of the text than sections i–x, and that the Notes on Manuscripts and passages of the text and the Bibliography are specially intended for classical students.

1. *Tacitus*

P. Cornelius Tacitus was born in a country-town of North Italy about A.D. 55 and died about A.D. 118. The son of a Roman knight, he himself rose to be a senator and passed through a normal senatorial career. He was consul in A.D. 97 and governor of Asia in A.D. 112–113. He was an intimate friend of Pliny the Younger. Both were successful orators, both distinguished men of letters. Pliny was proud to be regarded as a pupil of Tacitus and to be bracketed with him in popular repute. He addressed to him a number of his published letters—two of them giving a detailed account of the eruption of Vesuvius for the use of Tacitus in his *Histories*. Of the private life of Tacitus we know very little indeed. He married the daughter of Agricola in A.D. 77, but he never mentions her name.

The first literary work of Tacitus, *Dialogus de Oratoribus*, was written about A.D. 80 (or perhaps 100). The *Agricola* and *Germania* followed in 97–98. Then came the major historical works, the *Histories* (*c.* 104–112), covering the years 68–96, and the *Annals* (*c.* 112–118), taking up the story at the death of Augustus in 14 and carrying it to the death of Nero in 68. Both works have come down to us incomplete. Tacitus tells us that he had reserved for his old age the account of the happier age that followed the death of Domitian in 96. But it was never written. Did death overtake him, or had he lost the zest to write?

Tacitus was one of those Italians of the sound old stock, who brought to the service of the Empire a loyalty and a devotion that recall the best days of the Republic. It was the destiny of Rome to rule the world, the destiny of the high-born Roman to share in that great task; and Rome now meant not the city only, but Italy as well. We may think of Tacitus as something like an officer of the Indian army and an Indian Civil Servant rolled into one. He has a passionate belief in the 'career' as the one thing in life that matters.

The 'career' depended on the 'New Order' of the Empire, and men like Tacitus continued to pursue it under emperors good or bad. Tacitus himself had experience of tyrants like Nero and Domitian and of constitutional emperors like Vespasian, Nerva and Trajan. He reflected much on his experience, and ended with the sad conclusion that one must not expect too much. Autocracy and freedom could not finally be reconciled. The fact was that imperial tyranny pressed hardest on the senators. The tyrant forced the Senate to co-operate in his tyranny, and men like Tacitus, constrained to vote against their consciences in condemnation of their own friends, burst out into violent denunciations, once the tyrant was safely buried. This was natural enough, but it leads Tacitus to judge the Empire somewhat ungenerously. After all, it did confer on the world the great blessings of peace and order, and to Tacitus and men like him it opened up all that made life worth living.

Tacitus as a historian has several obvious defects. He is often amazingly careless about geography and military history. He is not deeply interested in the 'man in the street'. He is not always just, as, for example, when he hints, on very slight grounds, that Domitian poisoned Agricola. He permits himself an occasional sneer at the enemies of Rome, more suitable to cheap journalism of any age than to 'the majesty of the Roman Empire'. He mocks the Britons for adopting Roman civilization— poor, deluded slaves. He gibes at the Bructeri, butchering and butchered to provide a Roman holiday. He finds it 'glorious' that Roman legions should stand safely in reserve while their brave auxiliaries bear the brunt of battle. But he has great qualities. He has a lively imagination and a quick wit, he is manly and high-minded, and he is capable of genuine moral indignation, even if he occasionally spends it on trivial objects. There is enough in common between his age and ours for us to sympathize with his problems. The Roman Empire is, in fact, nearer to us spiritually than our own country in the Middle Ages.

The style of Tacitus grew under the influence of earlier writers such as Cicero and Sallust, but developed finally into something 'peculiar, pure and unique of its kind', like his own Germans.

Tacitus is fond of short sentences and shuns the long period. He is terse, fond of variety, given to inversion and poetic forms of expression. His works were probably all designed to be 'declaimed', read aloud, in the first place. That is why a chapter so often ends with an epigram; it is a signal for applause before the next chapter begins. Many of these epigrams leave their sting behind them.

But occasionally the form is there without the spirit. What Tacitus actually has to say is quite simple and not really epigrammatic.

I have tried to render Tacitus accurately and into natural modern English, but have freely sacrificed literal exactness to the claims of idiom. But we must not forget that Tacitus was a great stylist—perhaps the greatest of the Roman Empire—and that a translation is not really true to him unless it carries with it something of his sombre magnificence and his mordant wit.

II. *Agricola the Man*

The name of Cn. Julius Agricola, the father-in-law of Tacitus, is preserved on a lead pipe found at Chester and, under the form 'Aircol', in an early Welsh genealogy. But Tacitus judged rightly that it was his own story that would confer immortality on Agricola's memory.

To the details of Agricola's career, recorded in the book, very little need be added. The 'Julius' in the names of Agricola and his father suggests that an ancestor may have been enfranchised by Julius Caesar. The father wrote on the cultivation of the vine, and that possibly led to his son's being named 'Agricola' (farmer). The dates of Agricola's appointments were:

Tribunus Militum in Britain, A.D. 61.

Quaestor in Asia, A.D. 64.

Tribunus Plebis in Rome, A.D. 66.

Praetor in Rome, A.D. 68.

Legatus Legionis XX in Britain, A.D. 71.

Legatus Praetorius in Aquitania, A.D. 74–76.

Consul in Rome, A.D. 77 (? April to June).

Legatus Consularis in Britain, A.D. 77–83.

Life in retirement at Rome, A.D. 83–93, and death in latter year.

Agricola, then, had enjoyed a long and honourable career of public service. He had had the opportunity of acquiring an unrivalled knowledge of the province of Britain. He had a fine eye for the site of a fort, and he was an able tactician. But his strategy is open to serious criticism. His seven years of campaigning led to no decisive success, and it is even suspected that the Brigantes were in revolt when he left the province. His optimistic view that Ireland could be conquered and held by a single legion and a small force of auxiliaries makes the thoughtful reader gasp. Tacitus's description of his father-in-law (in Chapter 35) as 'an optimist who throve on adversity' is perhaps a little truer than he meant it to be; and we cannot refuse some sympathy to the 'cowards who pleaded for a strategic retreat' (Chapter 25), thinking that Agricola was asking for trouble by his bold dash into Caledonia. Domitian can certainly not be blamed for recalling him. Agricola had had a long innings, and troops were urgently needed at more vital spots on Rhine and Danube. Tacitus awards very high praise to the civil government of Agricola both in Aquitania (Chapter 9) and in Britain (Chapter 19). In

Britain too much was, perhaps, sacrificed to campaigning, for Agricola, as Tacitus admits, was in love with military glory (Chapter 5).

Agricola, like Tacitus, accepted the world as he found it. A good man himself, he was pained by Domitian's bad government. But he was reasonable and would not sacrifice his life in a useless defiance of authority. The refusal of Domitian to make any use of Agricola's services after his return from Britain was certainly prompted by jealousy and fear. But there was no real evidence that he poisoned him, and Tacitus might have acknowledged this more frankly.

Of Agricola's personality each reader must judge for himself. Tacitus certainly loved and honoured him, and convinces us that he had good reason for so doing. But there are few intimate, or even personal, touches. We are never told any anecdote of his life in camp or town, of how he dealt with such and such a troublesome centurion or won over such and such a Scottish chief. We meet rebel Britons, Roman soldiers, Caledonian champions of freedom. But we hardly see them except as masses. One wonders whether Agricola himself did. The portrait of Agricola, then, has power both to attract and impress, but it is rather the portrait of a career than of a man.

III. *Agricola, the Book*

The *Agricola* belongs to the class 'biography' and to the sub-class 'eulogy'. It is also a tribute to piety, for the object of the eulogy was Tacitus's own loved and honoured father-in-law. Such tributes to greatness have been paid from time immemorial. We need only mention the works of Xenophon, Isocrates and Plutarch among the Greeks, and Cornelius Nepos and Suetonius among the Romans. There were also two other Latin works— the *Bellum Iugurthinum* and the *Catilina,* of Sallust—which contributed much to the plan of the Agricola, even though neither of them is exactly a biography. Apart from literary works in Rome, there were also the funeral orations, customarily delivered over the illustrious dead.

The *Agricola* follows the common plan. In Chapters 1–3 the subject is introduced and explained, in Chapters 4–9 the life and career of Agricola are sketched down to his entry on the governorship of Britain. Then follows a digression—a description of Britain (Chapters 10–12) and a short history of the early conquest (Chapters 13–17). In Chapter 18 we come back to Agricola and follow his glorious career in Britain down to Chapter 38. The concluding Chapters, 39–46, describe his recall to Rome, his perils in retirement and his death—ending with the thought of his undying fame.

The *Agricola* was written in A.D. 97–98, probably begun before the death of Nerva and completed afterwards. Tacitus was already planning to write a general history of the years A.D. 68–96, and the account of Britain in the *Agricola* might be regarded as a preparative study. But it is the biographical interest that is always to the fore;

details both of geography and history are cut down to a bare minimum.

But was the *Agricola* something more than a biography? Was it a tract in defence of political moderation? There is some truth in the suggestion, but it must not be over-estimated. Agricola had certainly never opposed the tyrannical Domitian. He was a great man as far as he was allowed to be, but he knew when he must submit. For Agricola the defence may be accepted as adequate; but the charge of subservience could equally well be levelled at Tacitus and his friends, and here the defence is less successful. They had suffered in silence, voting against their consciences for the condemnation of their friends. They believed in the importance of their careers and felt no call to fruitless martyrdom. But they were trying to make the best of both worlds—to survive under a bad emperor and to resume full rank as patriots under a good one. Tacitus's own conscience is obviously uneasy. In Chapter 2 there is shame as well as sorrow in the story of Domitian's war on culture and merit; and in Chapter 45—the description of Domitian's final reign of terror—there is downright confession of guilt—'soon, Helvidius was to be led to prison by our hands'. The men who fell victims to Domitian were not all desperadoes, rushing on their doom; they included 'promptissimus quisque', all the 'live wires', one might almost say. The element of apology for the life of Tacitus and his friends is present then, but it is only a subordinate part of the book.

The *Agricola* has exercised a steady attraction on generation after generation of readers. The subject—the early history of our own island—has a strong natural appeal. The style never loiters, often sparkles, is never dull. Deep in the heart of the book lies an ideal that commands admiration—belief in Rome, in Roman destiny and in the Roman ways and standards of life. There is a note of tragedy in the thought that this ideal has to live in an unfriendly world, forbidden to reach perfection by the very conditions that enable it to live at all. And, throughout, a touch of warmth is added by the true affection that Tacitus bore his father-in-law.

IV. *Tacitus's account of Britain*

Britain was already fairly well known to the Romans by the time that Tacitus began to write. Even before 200 B.C. Pytheas of Marseilles had visited the island; he published some precious details about it, but was only called a liar for his pains. Caesar, Strabo, Pomponius Mela and others had added their quota to the account. Tacitus had the obvious advantage of close relationship to one who knew Britain as no Roman had ever known it before. But it is hard to take him quite seriously when he claims to have put research on a new basis, with solid fact to replace guess-work. He might possibly have done so had he taken more trouble.

Tacitus still holds the false belief that Britain was much nearer Spain than it actually is, and that Ireland lay between them. He accepts a false view of the shape of Britain. Certainly he could now for the first time state positively that Britain was an island—Agricola's admiral had confirmed the fact; but it had been the guess long before. It is hard again to understand how he can speak of the Orkneys as 'hitherto unknown'; 'unexplored' might be the truer word. Tacitus omits some details found in Caesar about the customs of the Britons—*e.g.*, their partiality for geese and their collective marriages—without troubling to correct them, if they needed correction. He never mentions the Druids, never says a word about the native British coinage, though it can hardly have been obsolete by his time. He has good accounts of the climate and of the deep inland penetrations of the sea in the North. But, though he frequently mentions estuaries, he never gives any detail that would enable us to identify one. He sends Agricola on expedition after expedition without once mentioning his base. He does not mention by name any of the chief Roman towns, such as London, Verulam or York. Writing for the special purpose of biography, he clearly omits much that must have figured in his *Histories*. But the achievements of Agricola, thrown on to so uncertain a background, begin to become blurred themselves. Tacitus writes as if any province, any provincials, any army, any enemy might serve equally well to illustrate his hero's virtues. Modern taste demands more precision.

v. *Britain before Agricola*

Modern archaeologists can tell us a little about the culture of Britain in the later Iron Age, but detailed knowledge only begins with Julius Caesar. That great conqueror, during his victories in Gaul, became aware of an unconquered Britain on his flank and decided to reduce it. His two expeditions—one in 55 B.C. a mere reconnaisance in force, the second in 54 B.C. a serious attempt at conquest—only won limited success. Had we any account but Caesar's own we should probably mark the second expedition as a failure. Britain, nominally subject to tribute, remained in fact independent. Augustus for a short time played with the idea of conquering Britain, but soon abandoned it for more serious projects. So our island remained free. But intercourse between Britain and Gaul was active and Roman influence steadily grew. Cunobelinus (Shakespeare's Cymbeline) for the whole of his long reign was a friend of Rome. Caligula in A.D. 39 gave a welcome to an exiled British prince and toyed with the idea of an invasion. But it was actually left to Claudius in A.D. 43 to carry out the enterprise. His motive is not certain. Britain was hardly dangerous to Rome and, if great mineral wealth was hoped from it, there was certainly disappointment.

The conquest was carried out without a hitch by Aulus Plautius. Claudius himself spent some days with his victorious army and was saluted as 'Imperator'. The South-East of Britain and Vectis (Isle of Wight) were quickly overrun. The next Governor, Ostorius Scapula (A.D. 47–52), conquered the Silures in South Wales, drove away the patriot leader, Caratacus, son of Cunobelinus, and enforced his surrender, when he fled North to the Brigantes in Yorkshire. By A.D. 49 the Romans had probably reached the Trent, Severn and Dee and were masters of Lincoln, Wroxeter and Chester. Colchester now became a colony.

Under Didius Gallus (A.D. 52–57) and Veranius (A.D. 57–58) there was no serious advance. Suetonius Paulinus (A.D. 59–61) ventured out incautiously from Chester on the capture of Anglesey, but was completely surprised by a general rising in his rear. It was led by Boudicca (Boadicea), Queen of the Iceni, who had bitter private wrongs to avenge. The rebels swept all before them and overran London, Colchester and Verulam. The cause of Rome looked desperate. But Paulinus, hastening back, brought the enemy to battle somewhere in the Midlands and retrieved everything by a single decisive victory. Paulinus was too merciless to the guilty, and the revolt dragged on. The government of Nero, therefore, showed true wisdom in replacing Paulinus by the gentler Petronius Turpilianus. He and his successors, Trebellius Maximus and Vettius Bolanus, ruled mildly during the years A.D. 61–71. The province as a whole was at peace, but the armies were mutinous.

Petillius Cerealis, one of Vespasian's ablest generals, displayed great vigour and made serious progress with the conquest of the Brigantes in Yorkshire (A.D. 71–74). Undaunted by his great reputation, his successor, Julius Frontinus (A.D. 74–77), broke the resistance of the Silures in South Wales, and probably advanced north as far as York.

VI. *Agricola's Governorship*

It was in A.D. 77, rather than the following year, that Agricola succeeded Frontinus in Britain. His appointment followed immediately on his consulship, and, if he was Consul from about April to June, there was time for him to be in Britain by late summer.

The seven campaigns of Agricola may be summed up as follows:

(1) A.D. 77. Defeat of the Ordovices. Conquest of Anglesey. The twentieth legion stationed at Chester (?).

(2) A.D. 78. Advance in the North along the western coast by a road driven from Chester to Carlisle. Garrisons placed between Solway Firth and Tyne.

(3) A.D. 79. Advance northwards by Eastern route from York, via Corbridge, to Tanaus—probably not the Tay, possibly the Tweed or Scotch Tyne.

(4) A.D. 80. Advance to Clyde and Forth and establishment of forts between them (Camelon, Bar Hill, etc.).

(5) A.D. 81. Advance along West coast from Chester to Solway Firth and Dumfries. Posts established

along the coast facing Ireland. Invasion of Ireland possibly planned, certainly not executed.

(6) A.D. 82. Advance into Caledonia. The fleet reaches Fife. The Caledonians attack forts west of the Tay and try to storm the camp of the ninth legion. Agricola establishes new forts—Ardoch, Inchtuthil, etc. A cohort of the Usipi mutinies and sails round Britain.

(7) A.D. 83. Agricola shatters the army of the Caledonian league at the Grampian Hills (Mons Graupius) in Perthshire—perhaps near Delvine.

In the next year, A.D. 84, Agricola was recalled.

Readers will observe how much geographical detail has to be added to make the account of Tacitus intelligible.

VII. *Britain after Agricola*

Tacitus tells us that Britain was 'completely conquered and then allowed to slip'. He evidently means that a permanent conquest of the whole island was now possible, but that the chance was missed. But that does not mean that all Agricola's gains were abandoned. Some of his forts may have still been held early in the reign of Trajan. Late in that reign a serious revolt broke out among the Brigantes, in the course of which the ninth legion disappeared from history. Hadrian drew his famous wall from Newcastle to Carlisle, and Antoninus Pius added his from Clyde to Forth along the line of Agricola's forts.

After that the island enjoyed a long peace. Septimius Severus (A.D. 208–211) renewed Agricola's attempt to conquer Caledonia, but the north of the island continued to be essentially free.

VIII. *The Army of Britain*

Britain was conquered by four legions—II Augusta, IX Hispana, XIV Gemina Martia and XX Valeria Victrix. There was also present a detachment of Legio VIII Augusta, and the whole force, including auxiliaries, must have amounted to some forty thousand men.

Of these legions there were still in Britain under Agricola:

> Legio II Augusta at Caerleon,
> Legio IX Hispana at York,
> Legio XX Valeria Victrix at Chester.

The fourth legion, II Adjutrix, at Chester (?), had replaced the Legio XIV in A.D. 70.

Among the auxiliary troops of Britain we can identify four cohorts of Batavi and two of Tungri that fought at Mons Graupius, a cohort of the Usipi that deserted and sailed round Britain, and, perhaps, at least one cohort of Britons. Tacitus does not mention the name of a single one of Agricola's justly famous forts. Quite a number, however, have been identified after careful excavation; a very useful account will be found in Anderson's introduction to the *Agricola*.

The legion II Adjutrix left Britain soon after Agricola.

About A.D. 115 the ninth legion*, as we have seen, was destroyed, and was replaced at York by Legio VI Victrix.

IX. *Germania, the Book*

Tacitus's essay 'On the Origin and Geography of Germany' was long ago hailed as a 'golden book'. It is certainly the best of its kind in antiquity, perhaps in any age. The genius of the author has stamped it with a character of its own; but, none the less, it follows a model that had gradually been developed over many centuries.

Here as always it is to Greece that one must look first. Hecataeus of Miletus, Herodotus, the great medical writer Hippocrates, and Aristotle himself had found time for the study of peoples. Coming to Roman times, we find Posidonius of Rhodes (*c.* 135–51 B.C.) devoting to Germany the thirtieth of his fifty-two books of histories. First among the Roman authors comes Julius Caesar, who allotted a few invaluable chapters of his *Gallic War* to the German peoples. Livy gave up the one hundred and fourth book of his histories to an account of Germany. He must have been able to draw on fresh sources of information, opened up by the campaigns of Augustus's generals in Germany. Strabo wrote of Germany in his seventh book; but he is thought to have been little known or studied in the West of the Empire. Pliny the Elder carried his *German Wars* down to about the death of

* 'It is now seriously questioned whether the ninth legion was destroyed as early as this.' (E. B. Birley.)

Claudius. It was obviously a work of the first importance, but it is completely lost. Pliny had served on the
frontier himself, and could depend on eye-witness, as well
as on the evidence of friends. Tacitus certainly knew and
esteemed the work of Caesar. Strabo, perhaps, was unfamiliar to him. Tacitus's debt to Pliny would probably
prove to be very great, could we assess it exactly. How
much Tacitus may have been able to add by drawing on the
experience of soldiers and merchants of his own day cannot
be exactly gauged, but it must have been considerable.

The date of the *Germania* is exactly fixed to A.D. 98,
the second consulship of Trajan. It is only a very little
later than the *Agricola* and, in composition, may even have
overlapped it.

The *Germania* is, as it professes to be, a study of the
character, customs and geography of a people. But is it
something more than that, a tract with a strong moral
purpose or a political pamphlet? It is necessary to ex-
amine these two questions before going on to a third one
—is the *Germania*, in general, reliable?

Tacitus unmistakably contrasts the virtues of the Germans, which recall the uncorrupted morals of old Rome,
with the degeneracy of the Empire. The Germans think
lightly of the precious metals. They love freedom.
Freedmen are kept in their proper place. Women are
chaste, home-life is pure, childlessness is not turned into a
profitable career. There are no insidious banquets, no
professional shows, no pompous funerals. Many a

biting epigram sharpens the contrast. 'The Germans do not call it up-to-date to debauch and be debauched.' On the other hand, they are not completely idealized. Their characteristic weaknesses are exposed—their indolence, their quarrelsomeness, their drunkenness, their silly passion for war.

The tendency to moralize, then, is a feature, but not the main purpose, of the book. The suggestion left on the mind of the reader is that, if the Empire should continue to relax in so deep a peace and if the Germans should add discipline to their valour, they would become a deadly menace to Rome. Tacitus was certainly speaking with the voice of history herself.

The Emperor Trajan spent the first year and a half of his reign in the two German provinces*, and was still there when the *Germania* came out. Tacitus obviously took advantage of the popular interest in those provinces. But was he venturing to recommend any definite policy, either that of the Emperor himself or an alternative one?

The policy of Trajan, possibly not obvious at the time, became so as his reign went on. The German frontier was to be firmly held, but there was to be no conquest of Germany. The strength of the Roman arms was to be directed against Dacia and Parthia. Now, what does Tacitus say? The conquest of Germany is taking so long —too long. All that Rome can now pray for is that her

* 'Upper' and 'Lower' Germany, military districts on the *left* bank of the Rhine.

enemies may be disunited. There is no suggestion of a
renewed offensive. The one allusion to the Elbe is just a
sigh of regret over a dream of the past. For all that, Germany cannot be treated lightly; unconquered, she remains
a constant challenge and a constant threat to Rome.

So far, the suggestions of Tacitus seem to point in the
same direction as the official policy, but they do not go
with it all the way. When Tacitus speaks of 'the fates of
Empire driving hard', he takes a far more pessimistic view
than Trajan could possibly have done. For Tacitus the best
is over; fortune has given Rome her choicest gifts.
Trajan showed by his actions that he judged the extension
of the Empire to be both possible and desirable. One
passage in the *Germania* reads like a deliberate criticism of
the policy which Trajan was later to pursue: 'The liberty
of the Germans is a deadlier foe than the tyranny of the
kings of Parthia.'

Tacitus, then, realizes the political interest of his subject
and gives fair expression to some of the considerations
that governed official policy, but he is *not* a propagandist;
and in any case the political aspect is subordinated to the
main theme.

To the question whether the *Germania* is reliable we
can give an affirmative answer. Tacitus is at fault here and
there; for example, he underrates the importance of
Roman trade with Germany and exaggerates the German
disregard for gold and silver. But his evidence on many
points—such as German armour and dress—has been

brilliantly confirmed by archaeological evidence. If he sometimes applies to the Germans phrases applied by earlier authors to other peoples, he does not borrow slavishly or in ignorance. Where the Germans differ, he is quick to note the difference.

The German people in the time of Tacitus was already a force to be reckoned with in Europe. We know to our cost that it has not ceased to be so to-day. Has Tacitus fairly characterized the Germans of his time? And do their characteristics live on in the Germany of ours?

Tacitus's picture of the Germans is vivid and self-consistent. They have a strong love of freedom, a keen sense of honour and a regard for the sanctity of home-life. They possess the military virtues, but make them look somewhat ridiculous by wanting to fight for any or no reason. In peace-time their standards relax abruptly. In fact, they are like adventurous lads, never quite grown up. They need Roman discipline if they are ever to reach maturity. Tacitus's claim for a unique purity of the race may be exaggerated, but is not altogether at fault. He never dreamt of the mischievous nonsense that he was going to suggest to later theorists.

What might the future of Europe have been if Augustus had held the Elbe frontier and made Germany a Roman province? Modern Germany has claimed to draw her strength from her ancient barbarian tradition, and has made a virtue of her late submission to Latin civilisation. She has glorified the natural man with all his virtues and his vices. The *Germania* has been brought into this movement. It has been assiduously taught in German schools and universities and made into a sort of Bible of German patriotism.

The population of modern Germany has certainly changed very considerably since the time of Tacitus. The real Nordic race must surely be sought first in Scandinavia, if anywhere. The National Socialist talk of 'Blut und Boden' was just mystical nonsense. One cannot really make heroic models out of the boisterous, overgrown boys that the ancient Germans were. All these appeals to ancient history to justify modern policies begin with self-deception and proceed to deceive others. Races do not remain pure over centuries. Whatever the fanatic may say, the disinterested student will have none of it. But climate does remain much the same over millennia, and can profoundly influence the character of peoples. Is it possible, then, that the 'Germanentum', the fierce sense of national idiosyncrasy, the 'Furor Teutonicus', may be something that really tends to grow in the various peoples that have successively fallen under the influence of 'Middle Europe'? Well, that will be one of the inevitable causes to which the fatalist will attribute the fall of Europe, if Europe really is to fall. But we have still the right to hope that more self-knowledge and more self-discipline can save Germany and Europe together.

At a few points Tacitus seems to be at fault—for

instance, when he denies that domestic slavery existed in Germany. His account of the German chiefs is quite correct, if we understand by 'chiefs' the men marked out by birth and wealth as natural leaders. To make them out to be magistrates raises unnecessary difficulties.

In several passages Tacitus speaks of 'the hundred' in idiomatic senses which modern scholars have found hard to understand, but the suggestion that he was misunderstanding the word 'hundred', meaning district, will not do. Neither in Germany nor in Anglo-Saxon England was the word so used till centuries later.

x. Germany and Rome in History

For long centuries the German peoples were pressed back in the North-West from Jutland to the Oder by the masses of Gauls, who were then superior to them in strength. The civilized world confused them with the Gauls. In time they began to roam westward, and the Tungri and other tribes established themselves on the left bank of the Rhine. Rome, however, never realized who the Germans were, until in 113 B.C. the Cimbri and Teutoni emigrated from their far northern homes and broke in upon Italy. They first appeared to the North-East, and won a great victory, then took some time to recuperate until in 108 B.C. they appeared in the Rhone valley and defeated the Roman Consul, Scaurus. Worse was still to come for Rome. In 105 B.C. two consular armies were destroyed at Orange. Had the barbarians advanced direct on Italy, no one knows what might have happened. As it was, they turned aside to conquer Spain, found the Spanish resistance unexpectedly tough and returned to Gaul three years later. Rome had had time to rally, and her best general, Marius, had given a new discipline and spirit to the army. The Barbarians divided their forces. The Teutoni were destroyed by Marius at Aix-en-Provence. The Cimbri, who had crossed over to enter Italy by the East, were crushed at Vercellae in the next year. The storm died down as suddenly as it had sprung up.

For over forty years peace reigned. But in 58 B.C. Julius Caesar found a new German menace in Ariovistus, King of the Suebi. He had been invited by Gallic tribes to help them against rivals, but soon took hostages and exacted tribute from his friends and kept drawing in new war-bands from Germany. Caesar picked a quarrel with him and drove him in rout across the Rhine. But Ariovistus had been accepted as a 'friend' by the Roman Senate, and Caesar's enemies in Rome accused him of downright treachery.

Again followed a long interval of peace. During the whole of the great civil wars the Germans made no move. Augustus, when he had won supreme power, turned his attention to the dangerous North. Not satisfied with the Rhine as a frontier, he decided on an advance to the Elbe. In a series of campaigns, directed by the stepsons of Augustus, Nero Drusus and Tiberius, the Germans were

ention of ruling as an autocrat led to his murder on the
us Ides of March (March 15th, 44 B.C.).

death of Caesar was followed by thirteen years of
attempt of Brutus and Cassius to restore the
Then the leaders of the Caesarian faction
it came to a

defeated in war and were gradually inured to Roman ways. It seemed to be only a matter of a few years before Germany was made a province. But the attention of Rome was distracted by the dangerous ambitions of Maroboduus, King of the Marcomanni, in the South-East. Close on this followed a desperate revolt against Roman rule in Pannonia. Germany was left in charge of Quintilius Varus, a nobleman devoid of military talent. He was ambushed and destroyed with his three legions in the Teutoburger Wald by Arminius (Hermann), chief of the Cherusci (A.D. 9). Augustus, brooding in bitterness, was often heard to cry out on Varus to 'give him back his legions'. Rome now returned to the defensive. Arminius himself, aspiring to kingship, was destroyed by his enemies at home. But he had done something most difficult. He had turned Rome away from a plan deliberately resolved on. From A.D. 14 to 16 Tiberius allowed his nephew, Germanicus, to make some amends for the disaster of Varus by displaying the Roman arms and paying honours to the Roman dead in the fatal wood. But the conquest would, obviously, cost too much. Tiberius decided to keep the Empire within its frontiers. Caligula suddenly conceived, and as soon dropped, a grandiose scheme of German conquest. The peace continued with hardly a break. But in the great civil wars of A.D. 68–69, a Batavian nobleman, Civilis, roused his countrymen and the Germans, under cloak of loyalty to Vespasian, against Vitellius. The Roman armies of the Rhine became demoralized and were destroyed. On the death of Vitellius in December, A.D. 69, Civilis should have placed himself at the disposal of Vespasian. But his head was turned. The Gallic tribes of the North-East broke loose from Rome and proclaimed an 'Empire of the Gauls'. The Germans naturally knew who the real masters would be. But Vespasian struck swiftly and remorselessly. His general, Cerealis, soon won a considerable victory, the Gauls of the South decided, on consideration, to remain loyal to Rome, and the rebels in the North began to waver. Civilis was content to accept surrender on reasonable terms. But Vespasian was inexorable in obliterating every trace of that ominous Gallic Empire. Vespasian and his sons tried to insure against future troubles. They closed the dangerous gap between Rhine and Danube, by occupying the 'Agri decumates' and drawing a military frontier in their defence. Domitian fought bitter wars on the Middle Rhine against the Chatti in A.D. 83 and 88. Though it was the fashion at Rome to deride his 'sham triumphs', modern archaeology has proved that his successes were not inconsiderable.

Trajan was in command in Upper Germany, when he was adopted by Nerva, and administered the two provinces from A.D. 98–99. It was probably in A.D. 98 that the Bructeri were nearly wiped out by their German enemies. Trajan left the frontier so secure that legions could be transferred from Rhine to Danube.

So far we have been speaking of the Western Germans.

With the Eastern Germans Rome's relations commenc[...] later, and were less intense. In 8 B.C. the Marcom[...] and Quadi drove the Boii out of Bohemia. Marob[...] the great Marcomannic king, gathered round hi[...] a confederacy as to excite Rome's suspici[...] But his glory exci[...]

ed
anni
oduus,
m so large
...uspicions (c. A.D. 6).
........, excited the envy of the other Germans, his empire collapsed and he finally accepted sanctuary at Ravenna in A.D. 17. The troubles on the Danube under Domitian were caused, not so much by the Germans, as by the Dacians and Sarmatians. The terrible wars of Marcus Aurelius against the Quadi and Marcomanni lie beyond our present scope.

History in the main has justified the forebodings of Tacitus. Germany, often triumphed over, was never conquered. The time came when no skill in defence, no valour in the field, no subtlety in diplomacy—when not even the discord of the Germans could avail. The fates of Empires at last pressed too hard. The barriers broke and the barbarian tides flooded in.

XI. *The Early Roman Empire*

The Roman Republic throve just so long as the Senate was able to direct and co-ordinate its policy. It broke down when the Senate lost control of its provincial governors, its generals and their devoted but rapacious armies. In the last and deadliest of the civil wars, in which the breakdown found expression, Julius Caesar won supreme power under the title of Dictator. His clear

int...
fam...

The ...
chaos. The ...
Republic failed. The...
partitioned the State between them. Finally ...
life-and-death struggle between young Caesar (Octavian),
grand-nephew and son by adoption of the dictator, and
Mark Antony, with his Egyptian wife, Queen Cleopatra.
The naval battle of Actium (31 B.C.) decided the issue in
favour of the young Caesar.

Octavian was determined to succeed where Julius
Caesar had failed; no assassins' daggers for him. He
'restored' the republic, but built into it a new position for
himself, thus founding what we have learnt to call the
Roman Empire. He established peace and order throughout the Roman world. He soon abandoned the idea of
conquering Britain, but tried long and earnestly to
establish a province of Germany on the right bank of the
Rhine. The failure of this great scheme has been described above. In the East he induced the Parthian king
to restore the captured Roman standards, and he asserted
Roman suzerainty over Armenia. The mere threat of war
sufficed to restore Roman honour.

As early as 27 B.C. he received the title of Augustus
(the revered), by which we still know him. His ever-
growing prestige was still more fully recognized, when
he was named 'Father of his country' in 2 B.C. But if his

work was to outlive him he must find a suitable successor, and to this end he laboured long and earnestly. First his nephew, Marcellus, then his great captain, Agrippa, then Agrippa's sons, C. and L. Caesar, adopted by Augustus himself, seemed destined for the succession. In the end, when all the rest had died, it was Tiberius, his step-son, who shared with him the burdens of empire and stood ready to take them over at his death in A.D. 14.

The long reign of Tiberius was marked by sound administration and sober foreign policy, based on that of Augustus. The renewed attempt to conquer Germany was abandoned in A.D. 17. Apart from that war and local risings in Gaul and Africa, the world enjoyed a golden age of peace. But at Rome Tiberius was never popular. Suspicious and uncertain of himself, he allowed the charge of high treason to be abused by informers against men of mark. And there was a constant struggle over the succession. Germanicus, nephew of Tiberius, died in A.D. 18, his own son, Drusus, in A.D. 23. In the years following, Sejanus, the powerful praetorian prefect, succeeded in poisoning the mind of Tiberius against Agrippina, the widow of Germanicus, and her family. Her two eldest sons, Nero and Drusus, were disgraced and put to death, and she herself died in exile. Tiberius meanwhile had withdrawn to the lovely island of Capri— to live, so rumour said, a life the reverse of lovely—and Sejanus was left to lord it over Rome. Still not content, he plotted against Tiberius. But the Emperor, warned just in time, struck first, and Sejanus fell (A.D. 31). Tiberius never returned to Rome, but died, loveless and despairing, in A.D. 37.

Gaius was the youngest son of Germanicus, taken into favour at the last by his great-uncle. He had been born in the camp and still bears the nickname of Caligula (little boot), given him by the soldiers. Having cringed to the aged Tiberius, he now delighted to play the tyrant, and, not content even with tyranny, affected to be a god on earth. His grandiose schemes of conquest in Germany and Britain ended in farce. He was finally murdered in A.D. 41 by an old colonel, whom he had made a practice of insulting.

Gaius left no obvious successor, and the Senate seriously debated a restoration of the republic. But the praetorian guard had found in the palace the middle-aged uncle of Gaius, the eccentric Claudius, and soon decided that he was not too eccentric for them. The Senate had no choice but to submit. Claudius was slow and pedantic, a slightly ridiculous character, but yet essentially able and conscientious. He carried through with complete success the long-discussed conquest of Britain (A.D. 43). He was derided by the Romans, not without some justification, as the slave of his wives and freedmen. His third wife, Agrippina the Younger, his niece, established a complete ascendancy over him. She induced him to adopt her own son by a previous husband, L. Domitius Ahenobarbus (the Nero of history), marry him to his daughter, Octavia, and prefer him above his own son, Britannicus. When Claudius died suddenly in A.D. 54, after eating freely of his favourite dish of mushrooms, Agrippina was with good reason regarded as his murderess.

Agrippina proposed to govern with her young son, Nero, but was quietly edged out of power by the young Emperor's advisers. To begin with, Nero was very popular and promised well. But he soon embarked on a terrible series of family murders—first Britannicus, then Agrippina, then his wife Octavia, whom he divorced, to marry the 'imperial whore' Poppaea. Under the influence of the infamous praetorian prefect, Tigellinus, he plunged into a career of debauchery, waste and cruelty. 'Rome burned while Nero fiddled', and the Christians were persecuted as though responsible for the fire. Foreign policy had its successes to show, a long war with Parthia carried to a triumphant conclusion and the British revolt under Boudicca (Boadicea) suppressed; a revolt of the Jews in A.D. 66 was still not quite crushed by the end of the reign. The declaration of the freedom of Greece was at least a grandiose gesture. But Rome was weary of the Emperor's misgovernment and profoundly shocked by that artistic temperament which drove him to appear on the public stage. Vindex, Governor of Gallia Lugdunensis, revolted, and Galba in Spain joined him. The German army under Verginius Rufus crushed Vindex, and the movement looked like collapsing. But Nero despaired of his own cause and retired from Rome into a suburb. On hearing that the Senate had declared him a public enemy, he committed suicide, murmuring as he died, 'What an artist the world is losing in me!'

A secret of empire had now been divulged: an emperor need not necessarily be made in Rome. Galba soon made his way to the capital, and was accepted without question. But he was old, he was mean, and he lost sympathy by unnecessary cruelties and by subservience to unworthy friends. At the beginning of A.D. 69 the German armies refused to swear allegiance to him and found an emperor of their own in the person of Vitellius, Governor of Lower Germany. Galba tried to prop his falling throne by adopting as his son a young nobleman, Piso. But in so doing he mortally offended another partisan, Otho, who had hoped for promotion himself. Otho bribed the praetorian guard, who promptly murdered Galba and Piso in the streets of Rome.

For most Romans the choice between Otho and Vitellius seemed to be simply one of two evils. It was the armies that decided, and the armies of Germany, led by Vitellius's lieutenants, Valens and Caecina, were too much for Otho's praetorians and army of Italy. The armies of the Balkans and Judaea had no time to intervene; for Otho committed suicide to save further bloodshed. But Vitellius was not left long in enjoyment of empire. Vespasian was proclaimed emperor by his troops in Judaea, and the Balkan armies joined him. A sudden dash on Italy by one of their captains, Antonius Primus, led to a surprise victory at Cremona over the flower of the German armies. Vitellius, betrayed by many of his friends, wished to retire; but bitter fighting broke out in Rome between his men and friends of Vespasian, and, when Primus forced his way into the city and decided the issue, Vitellius was murdered in the streets.

Vespasian showed himself master of the situation. He restored Roman prestige and recovered her shattered finances. It was hard that he should be called 'miser' for his pains. We have already seen how he suppressed the revolt of Civilis and the 'Empire of the Gauls' and, later, in A.D. 77, sent Agricola to Britain. From the first he marked out his two sons as his heirs. Titus was admitted to a share in the government, and even Domitian, the younger son, received the title of 'prince' (Caesar). Titus succeeded his father in A.D. 79, and was hailed as the 'darling of the human race' for his friendliness and generosity. But he died in A.D. 81, before his qualities had been severely tested. His short reign was marked by two disasters—a great fire of Rome and the eruption of Vesuvius.

Domitian was a man of great ability, but of cruel and difficult temperament. He allowed the charge of high treason to be revived for use by informers against his many political enemies, and made the Senate share in the odium of their condemnation. His wars against the Chatti on the Middle Rhine were not the failure that his enemies

made them out to be, but his later years were darkened
by long and difficult campaigns on the Danube against
Sarmatians and Dacians, ending in a not-too-glorious
peace. Agricola was recalled from his victories in Britain
in A.D. 84. In A.D. 96 Domitian, generally hated in Rome,
became suspect to his wife and his immediate entourage.
To save their own lives they murdered him and called
Nerva, an elderly lawyer of repute, to the empty
throne.

Nerva showed praiseworthy intentions of restoring
good government after the oppressions of Domitian.
Tacitus could hail his succession as the dawn of a new
age of liberty. But the praetorian guard, who had not
ceased to regret Domitian, demanded his murderers for
execution; Nerva pleaded, wept—and gave way. To
redeem his fallen prestige he adopted Trajan, the pride of
the army, as his son, and the disorderly praetorians were
soon brought back to their obedience. Dying in A.D. 98,
Nerva left Trajan to succeed unquestioned. Trajan's long
reign (A.D. 98–117) was signalized by the conquest of
Dacia and by a long war against Parthia, beginning with
brilliant success, but compromised at the last by a general
revolt of the Jews throughout the East. Early in the
reign of Hadrian his successor, Tacitus died. Whether
the high hopes that he had conceived in the first years of
Nerva and Trajan stayed with him to the last we cannot
say. The gloomy tone of his last work, the *Annals*, suggests that he had ceased to believe in that reconciliation of

autocracy with freedom of which he had so confidently written.

From Augustus to Nero the Empire was, as it were, the inheritance of a single family, the Julio-Claudian. Galba, Otho and Vitellius stand as isolated figures. The Flavian dynasty of Vespasian expired with the death of Domitian. With Nerva began that great line of emperors, succeeding one another by adoption, which gave Rome good government for a large part of a century. It might count as a substitute for freedom—to quote Tacitus's phrase— that emperors had now begun to be elected.

XII. *The Constitution of the Roman Empire*

For the Romans themselves the Empire was still the Roman 'Republic', 'The Senate and people of Rome'. But there was one modification, which to us seems vital. A number of powers were conferred on one man at the head of the State, sufficient to make his authority everywhere decisive.

The emperor, in the first place, was 'Imperator',* holder of the supreme right of command. The army swore allegiance to him, and to none other. In the second place, as holder of the tribunician power, he represented the Roman people and was personally inviolable. A 'law of Empire'† conferred on him a number of other rights, such as those of making peace or war, of transacting

* Hence our modern word 'emperor'.

† First attested for Vespasian, but probably earlier in origin.

business with the Senate—in general, of initiating any action that seemed to him proper. Such provinces as required armies were administered for him by his representatives; even in the peaceful provinces, which were left to the Senate, he had power to intervene at discretion. In Rome and Italy, which in theory were under the Senate, he undertook special charges, such as the charge of the corn-supply, of the night-watch, and, occasionally, of the public roads. In finance he came to exercise the powers of censor without the name.* He was sometimes especially entrusted with the supervision of public morals. He had his own treasury, the 'fiscus', and a special military treasury. He struck gold and silver coin in his own right; the coinage in base metal was administered by the Senate, but always under his supervision. He could administer justice in the ordinary courts as well as in a High Court of his own. The expressions of his will, given in edicts, dispatches and the like, came more and more to have the full force of law. As 'Pontifex Maximus' (chief priest) he was head of the State religion. While he lived, Rome sacrificed only to his 'Genius' (spirit); but in the provinces he was worshipped as a god. After death, unless his memory was condemned, he was 'consecrated', became 'divus' (the divine) and received full divine honours.

* Occasionally the Emperor *did* hold the censorship and might take to himself a private colleague. From Domitian onwards the censorial power, without the name, was regularly held by the Emperor.

To help him in his great task he drew on all classes of society—on the Senate for his chief provincial governors and generals; on the knights for his junior officers and financial agents (procurators); on the freedmen for the heads of such departments of his Court as finance, correspondence and petitions ('a rationibus', 'ab epistulis', 'a libellis'); on the slaves for the lower posts of his bureaux. As Senate and knights were so essential to his service, he found means of controlling the composition of both bodies.

The emperor normally tried to fix the succession by marking out a son or other close relative, or a son by adoption, as his political heir. 'Augustus' (the revered), a title conferred on the first emperor in 27 B.C., was borne by all his successors. 'Caesar', in origin the family name of Julius, was taken over by most emperors; but it was sometimes used to designate the heir or prince. 'Princeps' (chief citizen) was a common, though unofficial, designation of the emperor.

The Senate was taken by the emperor into partnership. It had the general control of Rome, Italy and the peaceful provinces, and, acting on the emperor's initiative, transacted a mass of public business by its decrees ('senatus consulta'). It administered the old State treasury, the 'Aerarium Saturni'. It even acquired powers unknown to it during the republic. It took over from the people the election of magistrates and sat as a High Court of Justice. It was the Senate alone that could make an emperor's position fully constitutional. The army could sometimes confer power, but never legitimize it. It was the Senate alone that judged the emperor's record after his death. Yet the partnership—the 'dyarchy', or 'rule of two', as it has been called—was always an unequal one; for in the last resort the emperor held the power of the sword.

The Roman people ceased to exercise its rights directly. It looked to the emperor to represent and protect it. A Roman satirist bitterly observed that its real requirements were two—'panem et circenses' (bread and games).

The old republican magistrates continued to be elected yearly. A man would enter the Senate as quaestor, would then become tribune or aedile, next praetor, and finally consul. The quaestors had financial duties in Rome, Italy and the provinces. The aediles were in charge of buildings and the police in Rome; the tribunes were still champions of the people, but were dwarfed by the emperor's tribunician power. The praetors retained only a part of their original legal functions, but were given the showy and expensive charge of holding the public games.

The consuls were still the chief magistrates of Rome, and the two regular consuls of each year ('ordinarii') gave their names to it.* The office was now limited to a few months, and many extra consuls ('suffecti') were appointed. By nominating and commending candidates the emperor

* The emperor would at intervals open the year as 'ordinary' consul with a colleague.

kept a firm control of elections. Prominent among the new officers created by the Empire were the prefect of Rome, a senator nominated by the emperor, and the prefect of the praetorian guard, a knight.

XIII. *The Provinces of the Empire*

The Roman Empire was divided into a number of spheres of administration or, as we still call them, provinces. It was in the main the creation of the Republic. The emperors consolidated it and rounded it off at the edges, but only rarely added new provinces.

The provinces where armies were required were governed by deputies appointed by the emperor, his legates, men either of praetorian or consular rank. There were other legates to command the legions, others to assist the governor in his duties. A financial officer—the procurator—attended to finance. A few minor provinces had no legate, but were under procurators who were also governors: such a one was Pontius Pilate, procurator of Judaea, under whom our Lord suffered. Egypt had its prefect, its viceroy.

The senatorial provinces—those that were peaceful and unarmed—were governed by officers appointed by the Senate—Africa and Asia by proconsuls, the rest by propraetors. The financial officer here was the quaestor; the procurator simply looked after imperial interests.

Every province was divided into 'dioceses' or administrative districts and 'conventus'—smaller districts in which the assizes were held. There were provincial councils to represent provincial interests, but they do not seem to have attained any great political importance. Taxes were either fixed as lump sums or as a quota, levied on natural produce. Collection was at first indirect, but tended to become direct as time went on. The burden of taxation was, according to ancient standards, not heavy. But there were also levies of corn and the like, often aggravated by cruel and absurd abuses.

Rome tended to rest her rule on the cities and, in the cities, on the moneyed classes. Some favoured communities became Roman colonies, others 'municipia'— that is to say, corporations organized on the old Italian model. A few cities—Athens, for example—remained nominally free. The population of the Empire cannot be closely estimated. It may have been about 40 million in the reign of Augustus.

Short notes on all the provinces mentioned in the text will be found in the Glossary.

xiv. *The Army and Fleet of the Empire*

The army of the Empire consisted of regulars, in the legions, and auxiliary troops. It was stationed chiefly on the frontiers, and served for defence rather than for attack. There was no field army.

The legion was a brigade—foot, horse and auxiliary services. It was divided into ten cohorts; the cohort was divided into three maniples, the maniple into two centuries. The strength of the legion was over 5,500 men. The legate, or brigadier, was a senator appointed by the emperor. Under him were ten commanders of cohorts—'tribuni militum' or colonels. The discipline and efficiency of the legion depended mainly on its centurions, sixty in number. The first centurion in each cohort was called 'primipilus', the first centurion of the first cohort, sergeant-major, was called 'pilus prior'. The badge of office was the cudgel of vinewood ('vitis')—not made only for ornament. The standard of the legion was its eagle ('aquila'). The maniples had their own special standards. The flag ('vexillum') was characteristic of cavalry.

The term of service was first sixteen years, raised by Tiberius to twenty. The age limits were seventeen and forty-six. The pay—ten asses a day—was raised by a third under Domitian. A special military treasury, founded in A.D. 6, provided for veterans. The legions were recruited from a few nearby provinces, later more widely. In theory at least only Roman citizens were eligible. Conscription could at any time be applied, but voluntary enlistment usually sufficed. Under Augustus there were twenty-five legions; by the end of the second century the number had risen to thirty-three.

The auxiliary troops were recruited in the provinces, chiefly in those that were new and war-like. They often used native weapons, but were usually employed away from home. They obtained Roman citizenship on discharge. The infantry were organized in cohorts of 1,000 or 500 men, commanded by colonels ('praefecti cohortis') of equestrian rank, the cavalry in squadrons of the same numbers, similarly commanded by colonels ('praefecti alae'). The auxiliaries received their keep, but nothing is known of their pay.

The garrison of Rome was composed of three parts. Its élite corps—the praetorian guard, concentrated by Tiberius in one camp in Rome—was recruited from Rome and Italy. It consisted of nine cohorts. Its commander (the 'praefectus praetorio') had under him colonels ('tribuni') and centurions. The pay and prestige of the praetorians were higher than those of the legionaries, their term of service shorter. The urban cohorts, three (later seven) in number, were under the command of a senator, the 'praefectus urbi'. Not all the cohorts were stationed in Rome; one, for example, was in Lugdunum (Lyons) as guard of the imperial mint there. The watch ('vigiles'), in seven cohorts, were freedmen, commanded by a knight (the 'praefectus vigilum'). Urban cohorts and watch had their own tribunes and centurions.

The fleet was decidedly an inferior service. The captains ('trierarchae') and men ('classiarii') were usually of free birth, but not Romans. The admirals ('praefecti classis') might be knights, but freedmen were sometimes appointed. The chief ships in use were the trireme and the fast light Liburnian galley. Italy had two main fleets, at Ravenna and Misenum, but there were many subordinate fleets throughout the empire—fleets of Rhine,

Danube and Black Sea, fleets of Egypt and of Britain. It was a Roman, Pompey the Great, who invented the great slogan 'navigare necesse est, vivere non est necesse' ('keep the seas we must, live if we may'). But few nations have done less than the Romans to live up to that motto.

In conclusion, it is my pleasant duty to give thanks for help received: to my colleague, Mr. C. J. Gadd, who made some valuable suggestions on the translation of the *Agricola*; to my friend Mrs. D. W. Brogan, who helped me with some useful notes on the *Germania*; to my old friend, Mr. J. W. E. Pearce, who has lent me his long experience and read the whole book in proof; to the General Editor, Mr. E. V. Rieu, who has, with fine discretion, used spur or rein, as required; to my wife, who has mediated between my difficult script and a puzzled compositor.

June, 1947   H. M.

BRITANNIA

English Miles
0 10 20 30 40 50

Legionary Fortresses
Forts
Forts certainly or probably
established before A.D 110
Large Towns
Small Towns (and modern names)

AGRICOLA

I

FAMOUS men have from time immemorial had their life stories told, and even our generation, with all its stupid indifference to the present, has not quite abandoned the practice. The outstanding personality has still won an occasional triumph over that blind hostility to merit that poisons all states, small and great alike. But mark two points of difference. In the past, the road to memorable achievement was not so uphill or so beset with obstacles, and the task of recording it never failed to attract the man of genius. There was no question of currying favour or grinding one's own axe. The consciousness of an honourable aim was reward enough. Men even felt that to tell their own life's story showed self-confidence rather than conceit. Rutilius and Scaurus told theirs, and were neither disbelieved nor criticised. How true it is that noble character is best appreciated in those ages in which it can most readily develop. But, to-day, as I set out to recount the life of one no longer with us, I have had to crave an indulgence which I should not have asked for an invective. So savage and hostile to virtue are our times.

2

Eulogies, indeed, were written by Arulenus Rusticus and Herennius Senecio—the one, of Thrasea Paetus, the other, of Helvidius Priscus. But both were treated as capital offences, and the savage punishment was extended beyond the authors to their books. The police, under official instructions, made a bonfire in Comitium and Forum of those masterpieces of literary art. So much is on the record. In those fires doubtless the Government imagined that it could silence the voice of Rome and annihilate the freedom of the Senate and the moral consciousness of mankind; it even went on to banish the professors of philosophy and exile all honourable studies, so that nothing decent might be left to vex its eyes. We have indeed set up a record of subservience. Rome of old explored the limits of freedom; we have plumbed the depths of slavery, robbed even of the interchange of ideas by the secret police. We should have lost our memories as well as our tongues had it been as easy to forget as to be silent.

3

Now at long last our spirit revives. In the first dawn of this blessed age, Nerva Caesar harmonized the old discord of autocracy and freedom; day by day Nerva Trajan is enhancing the happiness of the times; and the public security, ceasing to be merely something hoped and prayed for, is as solid and certain as a prayer fulfilled. Yet our human nature is so weak that the cure lags behind the disease. Our bodies, which grow so slowly, perish in a flash; and so too the mind and its interests can be more easily crushed than brought to life again. Idleness develops a strange fascination of its own, and we end by loving the sloth that at first we loathed. Think of it. Fifteen whole years—no mean fraction of our human life—taken from us. Many have died a natural death, all the most irrepressible have fallen victims to the cruelty of the Emperor. Even we few that survive seem to have outlived, not only our fallen comrades, but our very selves, in those years stolen from our manhood that have brought us from youth to age, from age to the far end of life's journey—and no word said. Yet even now I shall find some satisfaction, however unskilled and unpractised my tone, in recording the servitude we once suffered, and in gratefully acknowledging the blessings we now enjoy. In the meantime, this book, which sets out to honour my father-in-law, Agricola, will be praised, or at the worst pardoned, for the loyal affection which is its title-deed.

4

Gnaeus Julius Agricola was a scion of the old and famous colony of Forum Julii. Both his grandfathers were procurators of the Caesars—the equivalent of nobility in the equestrian order. His father, Julius Graecinus, was a member of the Senate and won fame by his practice of eloquence and philosophy. By those very accomplishments he incurred the wrath of Gaius Caesar; he received orders to impeach M. Silanus and, later, lost his life for refusing. His mother was Julia Procilla, a paragon of feminine virtue. Brought up under her tender care, he passed his boyhood and youth in a training in all the liberal arts. He was shielded from the temptations of bad companions, partly by his own sound instincts, partly by living and going to school from his very early years at Marseilles, a place where Greek refinement and provincial puritanism meet in a happy blend. I remember how he would often tell us that in his early manhood he was tempted to drink deeper of philosophy than a Roman and a Senator properly may, but that his mother, in her wisdom, damped the fire of his passion. It was only natural that such a fine and manly soul should be attracted strongly, if not too wisely, by the fair ideal of fame in its higher and nobler aspects. In time, discretion growing with age tamed him; he came away from philosophy with her hardest lesson learned—a sense of proportion.

5

He served his apprenticeship in the army to the satisfaction of Suetonius Paulinus, that sound and thorough general, and was picked by him to be tried out on his staff. But Agricola was no loose young subaltern, to turn his military career into a debauch; nor would he make his staff-captaincy and his inexperience an excuse for asking long leave with its relaxing pleasures. He got to know his province and be known by the army. He learned from the experts and chose the best models to follow. He never sought a service for self-advertisement, never shirked one through cowardice. He was always energetic; careless never.

Neither before nor since has Britain ever been in a more uneasy or dangerous state. Veterans were butchered, colonies burned to the ground, armies isolated. We had to fight for life before we could think of victory. The campaign, of course, was conducted under the strategy and leadership of another, and the decisive success and the credit for recovering Britain fell to the General. Yet everything combined to give the young Agricola fresh skill, fresh experience and fresh ambition, and his spirit was invaded by the passion for military glory—a thankless passion in an age in which distinction was misconstrued and a great reputation was as dangerous as a bad one.

6

From Britain Agricola returned to Rome to enter on his career of office, and married Domitia Decidiana, the child of an illustrious house. It was a union that lent him both distinction and material aid to his ambitions. They lived in rare accord, maintained by mutual affection and unselfishness; but in such a partnership the good wife deserves more than half the praise, just as a bad one deserves more than half the blame. In the draw for the Quaestorship he got Asia as his province and Salvius Titianus as his proconsul—and yet escaped being corrupted by either, though the province with its wealth invited abuses, and the proconsul, an abject slave to greed, was prepared to indulge his subordinate to any extent: 'You wink at my offences and I will wink at yours.' While in Asia he was blessed with a daughter, and his position was thus strengthened and his heart consoled for the early loss of a son and heir, born a year before. He passed the interval between Quaestorship and Tribunate of the people, and his own year of office as Tribune, in quiet inactivity; he understood the age of Nero, in which you were a philosopher if you lay low. His Praetorship ran the same quiet course, for no administration of law had fallen to his lot. Over the games and other vanities of his office he compromised between economy and excess, steering clear of extravagance but not missing popular approval. He was then chosen by Galba to check over the gifts in the temples, and, by his searching scrutiny, achieved a striking success; the State experienced no permanent loss from any sacrilege but Nero's.

7

The following year dealt a grievous blow to his heart and home. The men of Otho's fleet, while savagely plundering Intimilium in Liguria in their piratical career, murdered Agricola's mother on her estate, and pillaged that estate and a large part of her fortune. Her wealth had inspired the crime. Agricola had accordingly set out to pay the last dues of affection, when he was overtaken by the news of Vespasian's bid for Empire, and without a moment's hesitation joined his party. Mucianus was in control of the initial policy of the new reign and of the ordering of Rome; for Domitian was a very young man, and only drew on his father's credit for leave to enjoy himself. Mucianus sent Agricola to hold levies and, when he had performed that task with scrupulous zeal, put him in command of the twentieth legion. It had been slow to transfer its allegiance, and its commander was reported to be disloyal. As a matter of fact, the legion was a problem and a menace even to consular legates, so naturally its legate, being merely of praetorian rank, was impotent to control it: perhaps he was to blame, perhaps his troops were. Agricola was thus chosen, not merely to succeed, but to punish. But he showed a rare self-denial; he let it appear that he had found in his legion the loyalty he created.

8

Britain at that time was governed by Vettius Bolanus with a hand too gentle for a war-like province. Agricola reined in his energies and restrained his enthusiasm, for fear of trespassing on his chief; he was a master of tact, and had schooled himself to regard expediency as well as honour.

Soon afterwards Britain welcomed Petillius Cerealis, the
ex-consul. Agricola's worth now found scope for its dis-
play; but at first it was hard work and danger that
Cerealis shared with him—glory only came later.
Cerealis often divided the armies with him, to test his
quality, and when he had stood the test sometimes put him
in command of larger forces. Yet Agricola never bragged
of his achievements; as a mere subordinate he credited
every success to his inspirer and leader. Thus by his
gallantry in action and by the modesty of his reports he
evaded envy without missing renown.

9

On Agricola's return to Rome from the command of
the legion the deified Vespasian enrolled him among the
patricians, and then placed him in command of the province of Aquitania. It was a brilliant promotion to a post
important in itself and implying an expectancy of the
consulship, for which Agricola was in fact marked out. It
is a common belief that soldiers lack the finer points of in-
telligence; and indeed the law of the court-martial,
knowing no appeal and proceeding bluntly to its usually
summary decisions, gives no scope to the chicanery of the
law-courts. But Agricola, even in dealing with civilians,
had enough good sense to be natural and just. He made a
clear division between hours of business and relaxation.
When the assizes demanded attention, he was dignified,

serious and austere, though still inclined to mercy. When duty had had its due, he put off the official pose; harshness, arrogance and greed had long ceased to be part of his make-up. He succeeded where few succeed; he lost no authority by his affability, no affection by his sternness. To mention incorruptibility and self-denial in a man of his calibre would be to insult his virtues. The desire for fame is often a secret weakness even of the good, but Agricola never courted fame by advertisement or intrigue. Scorning all rivalry with his colleagues, all bickering with the pro-curators, he deemed it no triumph to override others, but ignominious to be overborne himself. He was kept in this command for less than three years and then called home to the immediate prospect of the consulship. Public opinion insisted that the province of Britain was intended for him, not because he said anything to suggest it, but because he was obviously the right man. Rumour is not always at fault; it may even prompt a selection. In his consulship he betrothed to me, in my early manhood, his daughter, a girl of rare promise, and after its close gave her to me in marriage. Immediately afterwards he received the command of Britain, coupled with the priestly office of 'pontifex'.

10

Though the geographical position and peoples of Britain have been described by many writers, I am going to describe them again, not to match my skill and research against theirs, but because the conquest was only completed in this period. Where my predecessors relied on style to adorn their guesses, I shall offer assured fact. Britain, the largest of the islands known to us Romans, is so shaped and situated as to face Germany on the East and Spain on the West, while to the South it actually lies in full view of Gaul. Its northern shores, with no land confronting them, are beaten by a wild and open sea. The general shape of Britain has been compared by Livy, the best of the old writers, and by Fabius Rusticus, the best of the younger, to an elongated diamond or a double-headed axe. Such indeed is its shape south of Caledonia, and so the same shape has been attributed to the whole. But when you go farther North you find a huge and shapeless tract of country, jutting out towards the land's end and finally tapering into a kind of wedge. This coast of that remotest sea was first rounded, at this time, by a Roman fleet, which thus established the fact that Britain was an island. At the same time it discovered and subdued the Orkney Islands, hitherto unknown. Thule, too, was sighted by our men, but no more; their orders took them no farther, and winter was close at hand. But they do report that the sea is sluggish and heavy to the oar and, even with the wind, does not rise as other seas do. The reason, I suppose, is that lands and mountains, which create and feed storms, are scarcer there and the deep mass of an unbroken sea is more slowly set in motion. To investigate the nature of Ocean and its tides lies outside my immediate scope, and the tale has often been told. I will add just one observation. Nowhere does the sea hold wider sway; it carries to and fro in its motion a mass of currents, and, in its ebb and flow, is not held by the coast, but passes deep inland and winds about, pushing in among highlands and mountains, as if in its own domain.

II

Who the first inhabitants of Britain were, whether natives or immigrants, remains obscure; one must remember we are dealing with barbarians. But physical characteristics vary, and that very variation is suggestive. The reddish hair and large limbs of the Caledonians proclaim a German origin, the swarthy faces of the Silures, the tendency of their hair to curl and the fact that Spain lies opposite, all lead one to believe that Spaniards crossed in ancient times and occupied the land. The peoples nearest to the Gauls are correspondingly like them. Perhaps the original strain persists, perhaps it is climatic conditions that determine physical type in lands that converge from opposite directions on a single point. On a general estimate, however, we may believe that it was Gauls who took possession of the neighbouring island. In both countries you will find the same ritual, the same religious beliefs. There is no great difference in language, and there is the same hardihood in challenging danger, the same subsequent cowardice in shirking it. But the Britons show more spirit; they have not yet been softened by protracted peace. The Gauls, too, we have been told, had their hour of military glory; but then came decadence with peace, and valour went the way of lost liberty. The same fate has befallen such of the Britons as have long been conquered; the rest are still what the Gauls used to be.

12

Their strength is in their infantry. Some tribes also fight from chariots. The nobleman drives, his dependants fight in his defence. Once they owed obedience to kings; now they are distracted between the jarring factions of rival chiefs. Indeed, nothing has helped us more in war with their strongest nations than their inability to co-operate. It is but seldom that two or three states unite to repel a common danger; fighting in detail they are conquered wholesale. The climate is objectionable, with its frequent rains and mists, but there is no extreme cold. Their day is longer than is normal in the Roman world. The night is bright and, in the extreme North, short, with only a brief interval between evening and morning twilight. If no clouds block the view, the sun's glow, it is said, can be seen all night long. It does not set and rise, but simply passes along the horizon. The reason must be that the ends of the earth, being flat, cast low shadows and cannot raise the darkness to any height; night therefore fails to reach the sky and its stars. The soil can bear all produce, except the olive, the vine, and other natives of warmer climes, and it is fertile. Crops are slow to ripen, but quick to grow—both facts due to one and the same cause, the extreme moistness of land and sky. Britain yields gold, silver and other metals, to make it worth conquering. Ocean, too, has its pearls, but they are dusky and mottled. Some think that the natives are unskilful in gathering them. Whereas in the Red Sea the oysters are torn alive and breathing from the rocks, in Britain they are collected as the sea throws them up. I find it easier to believe in a defect of quality in the pearls than of greed in us.

13

The Britons themselves submit to the levy, the tribute and the other charges of Empire with cheerful readiness, provided that there is no abuse. *That* they bitterly resent; for they are broken in to obedience, not to slavery. The deified Julius, the first Roman to enter Britain with an army, did indeed intimidate the natives by a victory and secure a grip on the coast. But though perhaps he hinted to posterity how the island might be won, it was not his to bequeath. After him came the Civil Wars, with the leading men of Rome fighting against their country. Even when peace returned, Britain was long out of mind. The deified Augustus spoke of this as 'policy', Tiberius called it 'precedent'. Gaius Caesar unquestionably planned an invasion of Britain; but his quick fancies shifted like a weathercock, and his vast efforts against Germany ended in farce. The deified Claudius was responsible for reviving the plan. He sent over legions and auxiliaries and chose Vespasian as his coadjutor—the first step towards his future greatness. Nations were subdued, kings captured, and the finger of fate pointed to Vespasian.*

14

Aulus Plautius was the first ex-consul to be appointed governor, and soon after him came Ostorius Scapula—both of them fine soldiers. The nearest parts of Britain were gradually shaped into a province, and to crown all came a colony of veterans. Certain states were presented to King Cogidumnus, who maintained his unswerving loyalty down to our own times—an example of the long-established Roman custom of employing even kings to make others slaves. Didius Gallus, the next governor, kept a firm hold on what his predecessors had won, and even pushed some few forts into outlying districts, so that he could say that he had extended his sphere of duty. Veranius succeeded Didius, only to die within the year. After him, Suetonius Paulinus enjoyed two years of success, conquering tribes and establishing strong forts. Emboldened thereby to attack the island of Anglesey, which was feeding the native resistance, he exposed himself to a stab in the back.

* Vespasian subsequently became Emperor in A.D. 69.

15

For the Britons, freed from their repressions by the absence of the dreaded legate, began to discuss the woes of slavery, to compare their wrongs and sharpen their sting in the telling. 'We gain nothing by submission except heavier burdens for willing shoulders. Once each tribe had one king, now two are clamped on us—the legate to wreak his fury on our lives, the procurator on our property. We subjects are damned in either case, whether our masters quarrel or agree. Their gangs of centurions or slaves, as the case may be, mingle violence and insult. Nothing is any longer safe from their greed and lust. In war it is the braver who takes the spoil; as things stand with us, it is mostly cowards and shirkers that rob our homes, kidnap our children and conscript our men. Any cause is good enough for us to die for—any but our country's. But what a mere handful our invaders are, if we reckon up our own numbers. The Germans, reckoning so, threw off the yoke, and they had only a river, not the Ocean, to shield them. We have country, wives and parents to fight for; the Romans have nothing but greed and self-indulgence. Back they will go, as the deified Julius went back, if only we can rival the valour of our fathers. We must not be scared by the loss of one battle or even two; success may foster the spirit of offence, but it is suffering that gives the power to endure. The gods themselves are at last showing mercy to us Britons in keeping the Roman general away, with his army exiled in another island. For ourselves we have already taken the most difficult step—we have begun to plot. And in an enterprise like this there is more danger in being caught plotting than in taking the plunge.'

16

Goaded by such mutual encouragements, the whole island rose under the leadership of Boudicca, a lady of royal descent—for Britons make no distinction of sex in their leaders. They hunted down the Roman troops in their scattered posts, stormed the forts and assaulted the colony itself, in which they saw their slavery focused; nor did the angry victors deny themselves any form of savage cruelty. In fact, had not Paulinus, on hearing of the revolt, made speed to help, Britain would have been lost. As it was, he restored it to its old obedience by a single successful action. But many guilty rebels refused to lay down their arms out of a peculiar dread of the legate. Fine officer though he was, he seemed likely to abuse their unconditional surrender and punish with undue severity wrongs which he insisted on making personal. The government therefore replaced him by Petronius Turpilianus. They hoped that he would be more merciful and readier to forgive offences to which he was a stranger. He composed the existing troubles, but risked no further move before handing over his province to Trebellius

Maximus. Trebellius was deficient in energy and without military experience, but he governed his province like a gentleman. The barbarians now learned, like any Romans, to condone seductive vices, while the intervention of our Civil Wars gave a reasonable excuse for inactivity. There was, however, a serious outbreak of mutiny, for the troops, accustomed to campaigns, ran riot in peace. Trebellius fled and hid to escape his angry army. His self-respect and dignity compromised, he now commanded merely on sufferance. By a kind of tacit bargain the troops kept their licence, the general his life, and the mutiny stopped short of bloodshed. Vettius Bolanus, likewise, as the Civil War still ran its course, declined to disturb Britain by enforcing discipline. There was still the same paralysis in face of the foe, the same indiscipline in the camp—only Bolanus was a decent man, with no sins to make him hated, and had won affection where he lacked authority.

17

But when Vespasian, in the course of his general triumph, recovered Britain, there came a succession of great generals and splendid armies, and the hopes of our enemies dwindled. Petillius Cerealis at once struck terror into their hearts by attacking the state of the Brigantes, which is said to be the most populous in the whole province. After a series of battles, some not uncostly, Petillius had operated, if not actually triumphed, over the major part of their territory. Petillius, indeed, would have eclipsed the record and reputation of any ordinary successor. But Julius Frontinus shouldered the heavy burden, and rose as high as a man then could rise. He subdued by force of arms the strong and war-like nation of the Silures, laboriously triumphing not only over a brave enemy but also over a difficult terrain.

18

Such was the state of Britain, such the vicissitudes of war that Agricola found waiting for him when he crossed the Channel with the summer half spent, a season when campaigning seems to be over and our troops tend to relax, while our enemies seek to profit thereby. Shortly before his arrival the tribe of the Ordovices had almost wiped out a squadron of cavalry stationed in their territory, and this initial stroke had excited the province. The war-party welcomed the lead, and only waited to test the temper of the new legate. The summer was far spent, the irregulars were scattered over the province, the legionaries were assuming that there would be no more fighting that year. Everything, in fact, combined to hamper or thwart a new campaign, and many were in favour of simply watching where the danger lay. In spite of all, Agricola decided to go and meet the threat. He drew together detachments of the legions and a small force of auxiliaries. As the Ordovices did not venture to meet him in the plain, he marched his men into the hills, himself in the van, to lend his own courage to the rest by sharing their peril. Thus he cut to pieces almost the whole fighting force of the nation. But he realized that he must not lag behind his reputation and that the success of his first enterprises would decide how much his other enemies would fear him. He decided, therefore, to reduce the island of Anglesey, from the occupation of which Paulinus had been recalled by the revolt of all Britain, as I described in an earlier chapter. The plan was hastily conceived, and there was no fleet at hand; the resource and resolution of the general had to take the troops across. Agricola picked out the best of his auxiliaries, who had experience of fords and had been trained at home to swim with arms and horses under control beside them, and made them discard their whole equipment. He then launched them on a surprise attack, and the enemy, who had been thinking in terms of fleet, ships and naval warfare, completely lost their heads. What could embarrass or defeat a foe who attacked like that? They sued for peace and surrendered the island; and Agricola, in a flash, found himself enjoying reputation and respect. Had he not, at his very first entrance to the province, deliberately chosen a difficult and dangerous enterprise, at a time usually devoted to pageantry and ceremonial visits? Yet Agricola would not let success tickle his vanity. He had kept under control a conquered people; he would not represent that as a campaign of conquest. He did not even use laurel-wreathed dispatches to announce his achievement; but his very refusal to recognise his fame increased it. Men gauged his splendid hopes for the future by his reticence over so grand a triumph.

19

Agricola, however, understood the feelings of a province and had learned from the experience of others that arms can effect little if injustice follows in their train. He resolved to root out the causes of war. Beginning with himself and his staff, he enforced discipline in his own household first—a task often found as difficult as the government of a province. He made no use of freedmen or slaves for official business. He would not be influenced by personal feelings, recommendations or petitions in choosing his centurions and men. The best, he was sure, would best justify his trust. He knew everything, but did not always act as if he knew. He could condone minor offences, but had no kind of mercy for major ones. Sometimes he would omit to punish and be satisfied by a change of heart. He preferred to appoint to official positions and duties men whom he could trust not to transgress, rather than punish the transgressor. He eased the levy of corn and tribute by distributing the burden fairly, and cancelled those charges, contrived by profiteers, which were more bitterly resented than the tax itself. The provincials had actually been compelled to wait at the doors of closed granaries, buy back their own corn and pay farcical prices. Delivery was ordered to destinations off the map or at a great distance, and states that had permanent quarters of troops close by them had to send to remote and inaccessible spots, until a service that should have been easy for all ended by benefiting a few scoundrels only.

20

By checking these abuses in his very first year of office, Agricola gave men reason to love and honour peace. Hitherto, through the negligence or arbitrariness of former governors, it had been as much feared as war. But when summer came and he had concentrated his army, he was present everywhere on the march, praising discipline and checking stragglers. Himself he chose the sites for camps, himself reconnoitred estuaries and woods; and all the time he gave the enemy no rest, but constantly launched plundering raids. Then, when he had done enough to inspire fear, he turned to mercy and proffered the allurements of peace. As a result, many states which had till then maintained their independence abandoned their resentful mood and accepted the curb of garrisons and forts; and so skilfully and thoroughly was the whole operation carried through that no fresh acquisition in Britain ever came off with so little challenge as this.

21

The following winter was spent on schemes of the most salutary kind. To induce a people, hitherto scattered, uncivilized and therefore prone to fight, to grow pleasurably inured to peace and ease, Agricola gave private encouragement and official assistance to the building of temples, public squares and private mansions. He praised the keen and scolded the slack, and competition to gain honour from him was as effective as compulsion. Furthermore, he trained the sons of the chiefs in the liberal arts and expressed a preference for British natural ability over the trained skill of the Gauls. The result was that in place of distaste for the Latin language came a passion to command it. In the same way, our national dress came into favour and the toga was everywhere to be seen. And so the Britons were gradually led on to the amenities that make vice agreeable—arcades, baths and sumptuous banquets. They spoke of such novelties as 'civilization', when really they were only a feature of enslavement.

22

The third year of campaigning opened up new nations, for the territory of tribes as far as the estuary named Tanaus was ravaged. Our army was seriously buffeted by furious storms, but the enemy were now too terrified to molest it. There was even time to spare for the establishment of forts. It was observed by experts that no general had ever shown a better eye for ground than Agricola. No fort of his was ever stormed, ever capitulated or was ever abandoned. They were protected against long protracted siege by supplies renewed every year. And so winter in these forts had no terrors. Frequent sallies were made, and every commandant could look after himself. The enemy were baffled and near despairing. They could no longer retrieve the losses of the summer by the gains of the winter, but were equally hard pressed in both seasons.

Agricola was never greedy in stealing the credit for other men's work. Every centurion and prefect found in him an honest witness to his merit. By some accounts, he could be very bitter in reprimand; and certainly he was as nasty to the wrong kind of man as he was nice to the right. But his anger left no secret residue, and you had no need to fear his silence. He thought it more honourable to hurt than to hate.

23

The fourth summer was spent in securing the districts already overrun, and, if the valour of our armies and the glory of Rome had not forbidden a halt, a place for halting was found inside Britain itself. Clyde and Forth, carried inland to a great depth on the tides of opposite seas, are separated only by a narrow neck of land. This neck was now secured by garrisons, and the whole sweep of country to the south was safe in our hands. The enemy had been pushed into what was virtually another island.

24

In the fifth year of campaigning Agricola began with a sea passage, and in a series of successful actions subdued nations hitherto unknown. The whole side of Britain that faces Ireland was lined with his forces. But his motive was rather hope than fear. Ireland, lying between Britain and Spain, and easily accessible also from the Gallic sea, might, to great general advantage, bind in closer union that powerful section of the empire. Ireland is small in extent as compared to Britain, but larger than the islands of the Mediterranean. In soil, in climate and in the character and civilization of its inhabitants it is much like Britain. Its approaches and harbours are tolerably well known from merchants who trade there. Agricola had given a welcome to an Irish prince, who had been driven from home by a rebellion; nominally a friend, he might be used as a pawn in the game. I have often heard Agricola say that Ireland could be reduced and held by a single legion and a few auxiliaries, and that the conquest would also pay from the point of view of Britain, if Roman arms were in evidence on every side and liberty vanished off the map.

25

In the summer in which his sixth year of office began, Agricola embraced in his schemes the states that lie beyond the Forth. Fearing a general rising of the northern nations and threatening movements by the enemy on land, he used his fleet to reconnoitre the harbours. It was first brought in by Agricola to bring up his forces to the requisite strength. Its continued attendance on him made an excellent impression. The war was pushed forward simultaneously by land and sea; and infantry, cavalry and marines, often meeting in the same camp, would mess and make merry together. They would boast, as soldiers will, of their several exploits and adventures, and match the perilous depths of woods and mountains against the hazards of storms and tides, the victories on land against the conquest of the ocean. The Britons, for their part, as was learned from prisoners, were stupefied by the appearance of the fleet. The mystery of their sea was divulged, their last refuge in defeat cut off. The natives of Caledonia turned to armed resistance on the grand scale, exaggerated, as the unknown always is, by rumour. Without provocation they attacked one of our forts, and inspired alarm by their challenging offensive. There were cowards in the council who pleaded for a 'strategic retreat' behind the Forth, claiming that 'evacuation is preferable to expulsion'. But at that very juncture Agricola learned that the enemy was about to attack in several columns. To

avoid encirclement by superior forces he himself advanced
with his army in three divisions.

26

As soon as the enemy got to know of this move they
suddenly changed their plans and massed for a night attack
on the ninth legion. That seemed to them the weakest
point. Striking panic into the sleeping camp, they cut
down the sentries and broke in. The fight was already
raging inside the camp when Agricola was warned by his
scouts of the enemy's march. He followed close on their
tracks, ordered the speediest of his cavalry and infantry to
skirmish up to their rear, and finally made his whole
army join in the battle cry. Dawn was now breaking,
and the gleam of the standards could be clearly seen. The
Britons were dismayed at being caught between two fires,
while the men of the ninth took heart again; now that
their lives were safe they could fight for honour. They
even effected a sally, and a grim struggle ensued in the
narrow passage to the gates. At last the enemy broke
under the rival efforts of the two armies—the one striving
to make it plain that they had brought relief, the other
that they could have done without it. Had not marshes
and woods covered the enemy's retreat, that victory would
have ended the war.

27

Fired with self-confidence and the glory of this victory, the army protested that no obstacle could bar its
brave advance; 'We must drive deeper and deeper into
Caledonia and fight battle after battle till we have reached
the end of Britain'. Even the conservative strategists of
yesterday were forward and boastful enough after the
victory. That is the crowning injustice of war; all claim
credit for success, while defeat is laid to the account of one.
The Britons, on their side, felt that they had not lost
through any lack of courage, but through chance ex-
ploited by strategy. With unbroken spirit they persisted
in arming their whole fighting force, putting their wives
and children in places of safety and ratifying their league
by conference and sacrifice. The campaign thus ended
with the temper of both parties raised to fever-heat.

28

That same summer a cohort of the Usipi that had been
levied in Germany and transferred to Britain committed
a crime remarkable enough to deserve record. They had
had attached to them a centurion and soldiers, to teach
them discipline in the first place and thereafter serve as
models and directors. These they now murdered. They
boarded three warships, constraining the pilots to do their
will. Two of these incurred suspicion and were put to

death, the third did as he was told. As their story was still unknown, they sailed along the coasts like a ship in a fairy story. But the time soon came when they had to put into land to get water and other necessaries. This brought them to blows with the Britons, who defended their property. Often successful, they were occasionally repulsed. They were finally reduced to such straits of famine that they first ate the weakest of their number and then victims drawn by lot. In this fashion they sailed right round Britain, then lost their ships through bad seamanship, were taken for pirates and were cut off first by the Suebi and then by the Frisii. Some of them were sold as slaves and passed from hand to hand till they reached our bank of the Rhine, where they gained notoriety from the circumstantial account of their great adventure.

29

At the beginning of the summer Agricola suffered a grievous personal loss in the death of the son who had been born the previous year. This cruel blow drew from him neither the ostentatious stoicism of the strong man nor the loud expressions of grief that belong to women. He had also war to help to relieve his sorrow. He sent his fleet ahead to plunder at various points and thus spread uncertainty and terror, and, with an army marching light, which he had reinforced with the bravest of the Britons and those whose loyalty had been proved during a long peace, reached the Graupian Mountain, which he found occupied by the enemy. The Britons were, in fact, undaunted by the loss of the previous battle, and welcomed the choice between revenge and enslavement. They had realized at last that common action was needed to meet the common danger, and had sent round embassies and drawn up treaties to rally the full force of all their states. Already more than 30,000 men made a gallant show, and still they came flocking to the colours—all the young men and those whose 'old age was fresh and green', famous warriors with their battle honours thick upon them. At that point one of the many leaders, named Calgacus, a man of outstanding valour and nobility, summoned the masses who were already thirsting for battle and addressed them, we are told, in words like these:

30

'Whenever I consider why we are fighting and how we have reached this crisis, I have a strong sense that this day of your splendid rally may mean the dawn of liberty for the whole of Britain. You have mustered to a man, and to a man you are free. There are no lands behind us, and even the sea is menaced by the Roman fleet. The clash of battle—the hero's glory—has become the safest refuge for the coward. Battles against Rome have been lost and won before—but never without hope; we were always there in reserve. We, the choice flower of Britain, were treasured in her most secret places. Out of sight of subject shores, we kept even our eyes free from the defilement of tyranny. We, the last men on earth, the last of the free, have been shielded till to-day by the very remoteness and the seclusion for which we are famed. We have enjoyed the impressiveness of the unknown. But to-day the boundary of Britain is exposed; beyond us lies no nation, nothing but waves and rocks and the Romans, more deadly still than they, for you find in them an arrogance which no reasonable submission can elude. Brigands of the world, they have exhausted the land by their indiscriminate plunder, and now they ransack the sea. The wealth of an enemy excites their cupidity, his poverty their lust of power. East and West have failed to glut their maw. They are unique in being as violently tempted to attack the poor as the wealthy. Robbery, butchery, rapine, the liars call Empire; they create a desolation and call it peace.

31

'We instinctively love our children and our kinsmen above all else. These are torn from us by conscription to slave in other lands. Our wives and sisters, even if they are not raped by Roman enemies, are seduced by them in the guise of guests and friends. Our goods and fortunes are ground down to pay tribute, our land and its harvest to supply corn, our bodies and hands to build roads through woods and swamps—all under blows and insults. Slaves, born into slavery, once sold, get their keep from their masters. But as for Britain, never a day passes but she pays and feeds her enslavers. In a private household it is the latest arrival who is always the butt of his fellow-slaves; so, in this establishment, where all the world have long been slaves, it is we, the cheap new acquisitions, who are picked out for extirpation. You see, we have no fertile lands, no mines, no harbours, which we might be spared to work. Courage and martial spirit we have, but the master does not relish them in the subject. Even our remoteness and seclusion, while they protect, expose us to suspicion. Abandon, then, all hope of mercy and at last take courage, whether it is life or honour that you hold most dear. The Brigantes, with only a woman to lead them, burned the colony, stormed the camp and, if success had not made them grossly careless, might have cast off the yoke. Let us, then, uncorrupted, unconquered as we are, ready to fight for freedom but never to repent failure, prove at the first clash of arms what heroes Caledonia has been holding in reserve.

32

'Can you really imagine that the Romans' bravery in war comes up to their wantonness in peace? No! It is our quarrels and disunion that have given them fame. The reputation of the Roman army is built up on the faults of its enemies. Look at it, a motley agglomeration of nations, that will be shattered by defeat as surely as it is now held together by success! Or can you seriously think that those Gauls or Germans—and, to our bitter shame, many Britons too!—are bound to Rome by genuine loyalty or love? They may be lending their life-blood to foreign tyrants, but they were enemies of Rome much longer than they have been her slaves. Apprehension and terror are weak bonds of affection; once break them, and, where fear ends, hatred will begin. All that can goad men to victory is on our side. The enemy have no wives to fire their courage, no parents ready to taunt them if they run away. Most of them have no country, or, if they have one, it is not Rome. See them, a scanty band, scared and bewildered, staring blankly at the unfamiliar sky, sea and forests around! The gods have given them, spellbound prisoners, into our hands. Never fear the outward show that means nothing, the glitter of gold and silver that can neither avert nor inflict a wound. In the ranks of our very enemies we shall find hands to help us. The Britons will recognize our cause as their own, the Gauls will remember their lost liberty, the rest of the Germans will desert them as surely as the Usipi have just done. They have nothing in reserve that need alarm us—only forts without garrisons, colonies of grey-beards, towns sick and distracted between rebel subjects and tyrant masters. Here before us is their general, here his army; behind are the tribute, the mines and all the other whips to scourge slaves. Whether you are to endure these for ever or take summary vengeance, this field must decide. On, then, into action and, as you go, think of those that went before you and of those that shall come after.'

33

This speech was received with enthusiasm, expressed, as barbarians express it, by shouting, singing and confused applause. Bodies of troops began to move and arms blazed, as the adventurous sallied out in front, and all the time their battle-line was taking shape. Agricola's soldiers were in good heart and fretting at confinement within their defences. For all that, he felt it desirable to put the final edge on their courage and addressed them thus:

'This is the seventh year, comrades, that you by your valour, by the divine blessing on Rome and by my loyal efforts have been conquering Britain. All these campaigns, all these battles, have made great demands—on courage in face of the enemy, on patient toil in face of Nature herself; but, in all, I have had no complaint to make of my men nor you of your general. And so we have passed the limits that held back former legates and their armies. Our grip on the ends of Britain is vouched for, not by report or rumour, but by our encampment there in force. Britain has been discovered and at the same time subdued. How often on the march, when you were making your weary way over marshes, mountains and rivers, have I heard the bravest of you exclaim; "When shall we find the enemy? When shall we come to grips?" Well, here they come, dislodged from their lairs. The field lies open, as you so bravely desired it. An easy path awaits you if you win, but a hard and uphill one if you lose. The miles of hard marching behind you, the woods you have threaded, the estuaries you have crossed—all redound to your credit and honour, while you keep your eyes to the front; but, if once you retreat, present assets become deadly liabilities. We have not the exact local knowledge that our enemy has, we have not his abundant supplies; but we have our hands and our swords in them, and, with that, we have all that matters. For myself, I made up my mind long ago that no army and no general can safely turn their back. It follows, then, that a death of honour is better than a life of shame, and safety and renown are to be sought in the same field; and, if we must perish, it would be no mean glory to fall where land and nature end.

34

'If you were confronted by strange nations and an unfamiliar army, I would quote the example of other armies to encourage you. That is not the case; you need only recall your own battle-honours, only question your own eyes. These are the men who last year took advantage of night-time to attack a single legion, only to be broken by your battle-cry. These are the Britons with the longest legs—the only reason they have survived so long. When we used to plunge into the woods and thickets, all the brave beasts charged straight at us, the timid and passive slunk away at the mere sound of our tread. It is just the same now. The flower of Britain has fallen long since; what is left is a pack of spiritless cravens. You have indeed got them at last; but you have caught them—they never meant to stand. It is only extreme danger and deadly fear that have rooted them to this spot, where you may gain a great and memorable victory. Have done with campaigning, crown fifty years with one day of splendour, convince Rome that, if wars have dragged on or been permitted to revive, her soldiers were not to blame!'

35

Even while Agricola was still speaking the troops showed visible signs of their keenness, and a wild burst of enthusiasm greeted the end of his speech. Without delay they flew to arms. The troops were mad for action and ready to rush into it, but Agricola marshalled them with care. The auxiliary infantry, 8,000 in number, made a strong centre, while 3,000 cavalry were thrown out on the flanks. The legions were stationed in front of the camp wall; victory would be vastly more glorious if it cost no Roman blood, whilst, in case of repulse, the legions could restore the day. The British army was stationed on higher ground in a manner calculated to impress and intimidate its enemy. Its van was on the level ground, but the other ranks rose, as it were in tiers, up the gentle slope. The space between the two armies was taken up by the charioteers, clattering on in their wild career. At this point, Agricola, fearing that the enemy with their great superiority in numbers might fall simultaneously on his front and flanks, opened out his ranks. The line now looked dangerously thin, and many urged him to bring up the legions. But he was always an optimist and throve on adversity. He sent away his horse and took up his position on foot in front of the colours.

36

The fighting began with exchanges of missiles, and the Britons showed both courage and skill in parrying our shots with their great swords or catching them on their little shields, while they themselves rained volleys on us. At last Agricola called upon the four cohorts of the Batavi and the two of the Tungri to close and fight it out at the sword's point. The manoeuvre was familiar to those old soldiers, but most inconvenient to the enemy with their small shields and unwieldy swords—swords without a thrusting point, and therefore unsuited to the clash of arms in close fighting. The Batavi began to rain blow after blow, push with the bosses of their shields and stab at their enemies in their face. They routed the enemy on the plain and pushed on uphill. This provoked the rest of our cohorts to drive in hard and butcher the enemy as they met him. Many Britons were left behind half dead or even unwounded, owing to the very speed of our victory. Our cavalry squadrons, meanwhile, had routed the war chariots, and now plunged into the infantry battle. Their first onslaught was terrifying, but the solid ranks of the enemy and the roughness of the ground soon brought them to a standstill. The battle now looked anything but favourable to us, with our infantry precariously perched on the slope and jostled by the flanks of the horses. And often a stray chariot, its horses panic-stricken without a driver, came plunging in on flank or front.

37

The Britons on the hill-tops had so far taken no part in the action, and had had leisure to note the smallness of our numbers with contempt. They now began to make a slow descent and envelop our victorious rear. But Agricola had anticipated just such a move, and threw in their path four squadrons of cavalry, which he was keeping in hand for emergencies. He thus broke and scattered them in a rout as severe as their assault had been gallant. The tactics of the Britons now recoiled on themselves. Our squadrons, obedient to orders, rode round from the front and fell on the enemy in the rear. The spectacle that followed over the open country was awe-inspiring and grim. Our men followed hard, took prisoners and then killed them, as new enemies appeared. On the enemy's side each man now followed his bent. Some bands, though armed, fled before inferior numbers, some men, though unarmed, insisted on charging to their deaths. Arms, bodies, severed limbs lay all around and the earth reeked of blood; and the vanquished now and then found their fury and their courage again. Indeed, when they reached the woods, they rallied and profited by their local knowledge to ambush the first rash pursuers. Our excess of confidence might even have led to no inconsiderable disaster. But Agricola was everywhere at once. He ordered the cohorts to rally, discard their equipment and ring the woods like hunters. Where the woods were denser, dismounted cavalry went in to scour them; where they thinned out, the cavalry did the work. But the Britons, when they saw our ranks steady and firm and the pursuit beginning again, simply turned and ran. They no longer kept any formation or any touch with one another, but deliberately broke into small groups to reach their far and trackless retreats. Only night and exhaustion ended the pursuit. Of the enemy some 10,000 fell, on our side 360, among whom was Aulus Atticus, the prefect of a cohort, who in his young enthusiasm was carried by the charge of his horse deep into the ranks of the enemy.

38

Night brought our men the satisfactions of victory and booty. The Britons wandered all over the countryside, men and women together wailing, carrying off their wounded and calling out to the survivors. They would leave their homes and in fury set fire to them, and choose lairs, only to abandon them at once. Sometimes they would try to concert plans, then break off conference. Sometimes the sight of their dear ones broke their hearts, more often it goaded them to fury. Some, it was afterwards found, laid violent hands on their wives and children in a kind of pity. The next day revealed the quality of the victory more distinctly. A grim silence reigned on every hand, the hills were deserted, only here and there was smoke seen rising from chimneys in the distance, and our scouts found no one to encounter them. When they had been sent out in all directions and had made sure that everything pointed to indiscriminate flight and that the enemy was not massing at any point, Agricola led his army into the territory of the Boresti. Summer was almost over, and it was impossible for operations to be extended over a wider area. There Agricola took hostages and ordered his admiral to coast round Britain. The forces allotted were sufficient, and the terror of Rome had gone before him. Agricola himself, marching slowly in order to inspire terror in fresh nations by his very lack of hurry, placed his infantry and cavalry in winter-quarters. At the same time, the fleet, sped by favouring winds and fame, took up its quarters in the harbour of Trucculum from which it had set out to coast all the neighbouring stretch of Britain and to which it now returned.

39

The news of these events, although reported by Agricola in his dispatches in the most exact and modest terms, was received by Domitian with the smile on his face that so often masked a secret disquiet. He was bitterly aware of the ridicule that had greeted his sham triumph over Germany, when he had bought up slaves to have their dress and hair made up to look like prisoners of war. But now came a genuine victory on the grand scale. The enemy dead were reckoned by thousands. The popular enthusiasm was immense. There was nothing Domitian need fear so much as to have the name of a subject exalted above that of his prince. He had only wasted time in silencing forensic eloquence and all that was distinguished in the civil career, if another man were to snatch his military glory. Talents in other directions could at a pinch be ignored; but the quality of a good general should be the monopoly of the emperor. Such were the anxieties that vexed him and over which he brooded till he was tired—a sure sign in him of deadly purpose; finally, he decided to store up his hatred for the present and wait for the first burst of popular applause and the enthusiasm of the army to die down. Agricola, you see, was still in possession of Britain.

40

Domitian therefore gave instructions that the external distinctions of triumph, the honour of a splendid statue and all the other substitutes for the triumph itself should be voted to Agricola in the Senate, coupled with a most flattering address; further, the impression was to be conveyed that the province of Syria, then vacant through the death of Atilius Rufus, the ex-consul, and always reserved for men of mark, was intended for Agricola. It was very commonly believed that one of the freedmen in Domitian's closest confidence was sent with dispatches offering Agricola Syria, but with instructions to deliver them only if he were still in Britain. The freedman, it is said, met Agricola's ship in the Channel and, without even seeking an interview, returned to Domitian. The story may be true, or it may be a fiction; at least it suits Domitian's character. Agricola, meanwhile, had handed over a province peaceful and secure to his successor. In order not to signalize his arrival in Rome by the publicity of a crowded welcome, he avoided the attentions of his friends and entered the city by night. By night, too, he went, in accordance with instructions, to the palace. He was welcomed with a perfunctory kiss and then dismissed, without a word of conversation, to join the crowd of courtiers.

Agricola was anxious to tone down the military reputation which so easily offends civilians by displaying other qualities. He drank deep of peace and repose. He was modest in his dress, an affable companion, never seen with more than one or two friends. The result was that the majority who usually measure great men by their self-advertisement, after a close survey of Agricola, were left asking why he was famous; very few could read his secret aright.

41

Often during this period Agricola was denounced to Domitian behind his back, often behind his back acquitted. His danger did not arise from any charge against him or any complaint from a victim of his injustice, but from the Emperor's hatred of merit, Agricola's own fame and that deadliest type of enemy, the singers of his praises. And, indeed, the fortunes of Rome in those ensuing years were not such as to permit Agricola to be forgotten in silence. One by one came the loss of all those armies in Moesia and Dacia, in Germany and Pannonia, through the rash folly or cowardice of their generals, the taking by storm and capture of all those captains and their cohorts. It was no longer the frontier and the Danube line that were in question, but the permanent quarters of the legions and the maintenance of the Empire. So, as loss was piled on loss, and year after year was signalized by death and disaster, public opinion began to clamour for Agricola to take command. His energy, his resolution and military expertness were universally contrasted with the general irresolution and cowardice. Domitian's own ears, we may be sure, were stung by the lash of such talk. The best of his freedmen spoke out of their loyal affection, the worst out of malice and spleen; but all alike infuriated an emperor who was so ready to go wrong. And so Agricola was driven headlong by his own virtues and the vices of others to where glory lay—over the edge of a precipice.

42

At last the year arrived in which Agricola was due to draw for the proconsulship of Africa or Asia; and, with the execution of Civica still fresh in memory, Agricola was not without warning nor Domitian without precedent. Agricola was approached by some of the Emperor's confidants with the straight question whether he meant to take a province. They began with somewhat guarded praises of the life of peaceful retirement, went on to promise their good services should Agricola care to decline, and finally, throwing off the mask, pleaded and threatened in direct terms—until he was ready to go with them to Domitian. The Emperor had his hypocrite's part prepared. He put on a majestic air, listened to Agricola's request to be excused, and, after granting it, allowed Agricola to thank him, with never a blush for so odious a concession. He did not, however, assign him the proconsular salary, usually offered in such cases and given by himself in some—perhaps from annoyance that Agricola had not asked for it, perhaps out of very shame, not wishing to appear to have bought an abstention which he had imposed. It is a sin peculiar to man to hate his victim. Yet even Domitian, prone as he was to plunge into fury and only the more inexorable if he tried to hide it, was appeased by the measured wisdom of Agricola, who declined, by a defiant and futile parade of freedom, to court the fame that must mean his fall. Let it be clear to those who insist on admiring insubordination that even under bad emperors men can be great, and that a decent regard for authority, if backed by ability and energy, can reach that peak of honour that many have stormed by precipitous paths, winning fame, without serving their country, by a melodramatic death.

43

The end of his life was, of course, a bitter blow to us, his kindred, and a sorrow to his friends; but it deeply affected others outside his circle and even complete strangers. The masses and the commons of Rome, usually so bent on their own concerns, flocked to his house to enquire and gossiped in the markets and clubs. When his death was announced there was no one to exult, no one to forget too readily. The sense of pity was quickened by the persistent rumour that he had been poisoned. We have no definite evidence—that is all that

I can say for certain. I must add, however, that throughout the whole of his illness there were more visits from prominent freedmen and Court physicians than is usual even with emperors, whose visits are regularly paid by proxy. Perhaps it meant genuine concern, perhaps mere espionage. On the day of his death the critical stages of his decline were certainly reported by a line of couriers, and no one could believe that tidings need be brought so quickly if they were unwelcome. However, Domitian made a decent show of genuine sorrow; he was relieved of the need to hate, and he could always hide satisfaction more convincingly than fear. It is quite certain that he was genuinely delighted when Agricola's will was read in public; he left Domitian as co-heir with his good wife and loving daughter. Domitian took it as a deliberate compliment. His soul was so blinded and corrupted by incessant flattery that he could not realize that no good father makes any emperor but a bad one his heir.

44

Agricola was born on June 13th in the third consulship of Gaius Caesar; he died in his fifty-fourth year on August 23rd in the consulship of Collega and Priscinus. Should posterity care to know what he looked like, he was attractive rather than impressive. There was a lack of forcefulness in his features, but abundant charm of expression. You could see at a glance that he was a good man, you were tempted to believe him a great one. Cut off though he was in the middle of a life of splendid promise, measured by glory his life was absolutely complete. He had wholly realized those true blessings which reside in a man's own character. He had held the consulship, he bore the ornaments of triumph; what more could fortune contrive for him? He had no taste for vast wealth, whilst a handsome competence had fallen to his lot. We may count him blessed, then, who left a widow and daughter to survive him, who, in the full enjoyment of his great position, at the height of his fame, leaving kinsmen and friends secure, escaped by death from the wrath that was to come. Happy he, had he been permitted to see the dawn of this blessed age and the principate of Trajan, a prospect of which he often spoke to us in wistful prophecy! Yet it was no small consolation for his untimely loss that he missed those final days, when Domitian no longer left interval or breathing space, but, with a succession of blows so continuous as to give the effect of one, drained the last strength of the Roman state.

45

Agricola did not live to see the senate-house under siege, the senators hedged in by soldiers, and that one fell stroke that sent so many a consular to death, so many a noble lady to exile or flight. A single victory was all that was yet credited to Carus Mettius, the screech of Messalinus was still confined to debate in the Alban fortress and Massa Baebius was at that very moment in the dock. Soon, Helvidius was to be led to prison by our hands, we were to send Mauricus and Rusticus to their several fates, Senecio was to drench us with his innocent blood. Even Nero forbore to witness the abominations he ordered. Under Domitian more than half our wretchedness consisted in watching and being watched, while our very sighs were scored against us, and the blanched faces of us all were revealed in deadly contrast to that one scowling blush behind which Domitian sheltered against shame.

Happy you, Agricola, in your glorious life, but no less happy in your timely death. We have the testimony of those who enjoyed your conversation at the last that you met death with a cheerful courage. You seemed glad to be doing your best to spare Domitian the guilt of killing you. But your daughter and I have suffered more than the pang of a father's loss; we still grieve that we could not tend your illness, cheer your failing powers and take our fill of fond look and embrace. We could not have failed to catch some words of admonition to be engraved forever in our hearts. It was our special sorrow, our peculiar hurt, that through the accident of our long absence from Rome we had lost him four years before he died. All, more than all, dear Father, was assuredly done to honour you by the devoted wife at your side; but there were tears due to you that were not shed and, as the night fell, there was something for which your closing eyes looked in vain.

46

If there is any mansion for the spirits of the just, if, as the wise aver, great souls do not perish with the body, quiet, O Father, be your rest! May you call us, your household, from feeble regrets and unmanly mourning to contemplate your virtues, in presence of which sorrow and lamentation become a sin! May we honour you in better ways—by our admiration, by our undying praise, even, if our powers permit, by following your example! That is the true honour, the true affection of souls knit close to yours. To your daughter and widow I would suggest that they revere the memory of a father and a husband by continually pondering his deeds and sayings, and by cherishing his spiritual, above his physical, presence. Not that I would place an absolute ban on likenesses of marble or of bronze. But the image of the human face, like that face itself, is feeble and perishable, whereas the essence of the soul is eternal, never to be caught and expressed by the material and skill of a stranger, but only by you in your own living. All in Agricola that won our love and admiration abides and shall abide in the hearts of men, through endless ages, in the chronicles of fame. Many of the great men of old will be drowned in oblivion, their name and fame forgotten. Agricola's story has been told to posterity and by that he will live.

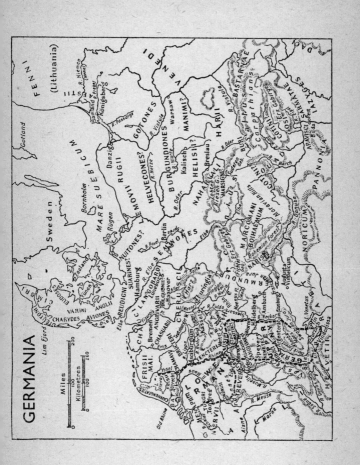

GERMANIA

I

THE country we know under the name of Germany is separated from Gaul, on the one hand, and from Rhaetia and Pannonia, on the other, by the rivers Rhine and Danube, from Sarmatia and Dacia by the barrier of mutual fear or mountain ranges. Its northern coasts, with their broad promontories and vast islands beyond, are lapped by Ocean. It is only in recent times that war has revealed the existence there of nations and kings unknown before. The Rhine rises in a remote and precipitous peak of the Rhaetian Alps and bends gently westward to lose itself in the northern ocean. The Danube flows from a gentle grassy slope of Mount Abnoba and passes more peoples than the Rhine in its course, before it discharges by six channels into the Black Sea. Its seventh mouth is swallowed up in marshes.

2

The Germans themselves, I am inclined to think, are natives of the soil and extremely little affected by immigration or friendly intercourse with other nations. For, in ancient times, if you wished to change your habitat, you travelled by sea and not by land; and the vast ocean that lies beyond and, so to speak, defies intruders, is seldom

visited by ships from our world. Besides—to say nothing
of the perils of a wild and unknown sea—who would
leave Asia, Africa or Italy to visit Germany, with its un-
lovely scenery, its bitter climate, its general dreariness to
sense and eye, unless it were his home?

In their ancient songs, their only form of recorded
history, the Germans celebrate the earth-born god,
Tuisto. They assign to him a son, Mannus, the author of
their race, and to Mannus three sons, their founders,
after whom the people nearest Ocean are named Ingaevones, those of the centre Herminones, the remainder
Istaevones. The remote past invites guesswork, and so
some authorities record more sons of the god and more
national names, such as Marsi, Gambrivii, Suebi and
Vandilici; and the names are indeed genuine and ancient.
As for the name of Germany, it is quite a modern coinage,
they say. The first people to cross the Rhine and oust the
Gauls are now called Tungri, but were then called Germans. It was the name of this tribe, not that of a nation,
that gradually came into general use. And so, in the first
place, they were all called Germans after the conquerors
because of the terror these inspired, and finally adopted
and applied the new name to themselves.

3

Hercules, among others, is said to have visited them,
and they chant his praises before those of other heroes on

their way into battle. They have also a different kind of chant. Its recital—*barritus*, to use their own name—serves to kindle their courage and helps them by its sound to forecast the issue of the coming battle. They inspire or feel terror according to which army roars the louder, and they regard the competition as one of valour rather than voice. What they aim at most is a harsh tone and hoarse murmur, and so they put their shields before their mouths, in order to make the voice swell fuller and deeper as it echoes back. Ulysses, too, in those long and fabled wanderings of his, is thought by some to have reached this ocean, visited the German lands and founded and named Asciburgium, a place still inhabited to-day on the banks of the Rhine. They even add that an altar, consecrated by Ulysses and giving also the name of his father, Laertes, was found long since on the same spot, and that certain monuments on barrows, inscribed with Greek letters, are still to be seen on the borders of Germany and Rhaetia. I am not disposed either to sustain or refute such assertions by evidence; my readers may believe or disbelieve at their own discretion.

4

For myself I accept the view that the peoples of Germany have never been tainted by intermarriage with other peoples, and stand out as a nation peculiar, pure and unique of its kind. Hence the physical type, if one may generalize at all about so vast a population, is everywhere the same—wild, blue eyes, reddish hair and huge frames that excel only in violent effort. They have no corresponding power to endure hard work and exertion, and have little capacity to bear thirst and heat; but their climate and soil *have* taught them to bear cold and hunger.

5

The country in general, while varying somewhat in character, either bristles with woods or festers with swamps. It is wetter where it faces Gaul, windier where it faces Noricum and Pannonia. Though fertile in grain crops, it is unkind to fruit trees. It is rich in flocks, but they are for the most part undersized. Even the cattle lack the splendid brows that are their natural glory. It is numbers that please, numbers that constitute their only, their darling, form of wealth. Heaven has denied them gold and silver—shall I say in mercy or in wrath? But I would not go so far as to assert that Germany has no lodes of silver and gold. Who has ever prospected for them? The Germans take less than the normal pleasure in owning and using them. One may see among them silver vessels, which have been given as presents to their envoys and chiefs, as lightly esteemed as earthenware. The Germans nearest us do, however, value gold and silver for their use in trade, and recognize and prefer certain types of Roman money. The peoples of the interior, truer to the plain old ways, employ barter. They like money that is old and familiar, denarii with the notched edge and the type of the two-horse chariot. Another point is that they try to get silver in preference to gold. They have no predilection for the metal, but find plenty of silver change more serviceable in buying cheap and common goods.

6

There is not even any great abundance of iron, as may be inferred from the character of their weapons. Only a very few use swords or lances. The spears that they carry —*frameae* is the native word—have short and narrow heads, but are so sharp and easy to handle, that the same weapon serves at need for close or distant fighting. The horseman asks no more than his shield and spear, but the infantry have also javelins to shower, several per man, and can hurl them to a great distance; for they are either naked or only lightly clad in their cloaks. There is nothing ostentatious in their turn-out. Only the shields are picked out with carefully selected colours. Few have breast-plates; only here and there will you see a helmet of metal or hide. Their horses are not distinguished either for beauty or for speed, nor are they trained in Roman fashion to execute various turns. They ride them straight ahead or with a single swing to the right, keeping the wheeling line so perfect that no one drops behind the rest. On a general survey, their strength is seen to lie rather in their infantry, and that is why they combine the two arms in battle. The men whom they select from the whole force and station in the van are fleet of foot and fit admirably into cavalry action. The number of these select men is exactly fixed. A hundred are drawn from each district, and 'the hundred' is the name they bear at home. What began as a mere number ends as a title of distinction. The line is made up of wedge formations. To retreat, provided that you return to the attack, is considered crafty rather than cowardly. They bring in the bodies of the fallen even when the battle hangs in the balance. To throw away one's shield is the supreme disgrace; the guilty wretch is debarred from sacrifice or council. Men have often survived battle only to end their shame by hanging themselves.

7

They choose their kings for their noble birth, their leaders for their valour. The power even of the kings is not absolute or arbitrary. As for the leaders, it is their example rather than their authority that wins them special admiration—for their energy, their distinction, or their presence in the van of fight. Capital punishment, imprisonment and even flogging are allowed to none but the priests, and are not inflicted merely as punishments or on the leaders' orders, but in obedience to the god whom they believe to preside over battle. They also carry into the fray figures and emblems taken from their sacred groves. Not chance or the accident of mustering makes the troop or wedge, but family and friendship, and this is a very powerful incitement to valour. A man's dearest possessions are at hand; he can hear close to him the laments of his women and the wailing of his children. These are the witnesses that a man reverences most, to them he looks for his highest praise. The men take their wounds to their mothers and wives, and the latter are not afraid of counting and examining the blows, and bring food and encouragement to the fighting men.

8

It stands on record that armies wavering on the point of collapse have been restored by the women. They have pleaded heroically with their men, thrusting their bosoms before them and forcing them to realize the imminent prospect of their enslavement—a fate which they fear more desperately for their women than for themelves. It is even found that you can secure a surer hold on a state if you demand among the hostages girls of noble family. More than this, they believe that there resides in women an element of holiness and prophecy, and so they do not scorn to ask their advice or lightly disregard their replies. In the reign of the deified Vespasian we saw Veleda long honoured by many Germans as a divinity, whilst even earlier they showed a similar reverence for Aurinia and

others, a reverence untouched by flattery or any pretence
of turning women into goddesses.

9

Above all gods they worship Mercury, and count it no
sin to win his favour on certain days by human sacrifices.
They appease Hercules and Mars with the beasts normally
allowed. Some of the Suebi sacrifice to Isis also. I cannot
determine the origin and meaning of this foreign cult,
but her emblem, made in the form of a light war-vessel,
proves that her worship came in from abroad. They do
not, however, deem it consistent with the divine majesty
to imprison their gods within walls or represent them with
anything like human features. Their holy places are the
woods and groves, and they call by the name of god that
hidden presence which is seen only by the eye of reverence.

10

For auspices and the casting of lots they have the highest
possible regard. Their procedure in casting lots is uniform.
They break off a branch of a fruit-tree and slice it into
strips; they distinguish these by certain runes and throw
them, as random chance will have it, on to a white cloth.
Then the priest of the State if the consultation is a public
one, the father of the family if it is private, after a prayer
to the gods and an intent gaze heavenward, picks up

three, one at a time, and reads their meaning from the runes scored on them. If the lots forbid an enterprise, there can be no further consultation that day; if they allow it, further confirmation by auspices is required. Their practice of questioning the notes and flights of birds is, of course, known also to us; peculiar to the Germans is the seeking of presentiments and warnings from horses. These horses are kept at the public expense in those sacred woods and groves that I have already mentioned; they are pure white and undefiled by work for man. The priest or king or chief of the State yokes them to a sacred chariot and goes along with them, noting their neighings and snortings. No form of auspices inspires greater trust, not only among the commons, but even among the nobles and priests. They themselves are only the servants, the horses are the confidants of the gods. There is yet another kind of auspices used to forecast the issue of serious wars. They somehow or other contrive to secure a captive from the nation with which they are at war and match him against a champion of their own, each armed in native style. The victory of one or the other is taken as a test case.

II

On matters of minor importance only the chiefs debate, on major affairs the whole community; but, even where the commons have the decision, the case is carefully considered in advance by the chiefs. Except in case of accident or emergency they assemble on fixed days, when the moon is either crescent or nearing her full orb. These, they hold, are the most auspicious times for embarking on any new enterprise. They count, not like us, by days, but by nights. It is by nights that they fix dates or make appointments. Night is regarded as ushering in the day. It is a defect of their freedom that they do not assemble at once or in obedience to orders, but waste two or three days in their dilatory gathering. When the mass so decide, they take their seats fully armed. Silence is then demanded by the priests, who on that occasion have also power to enforce obedience. Then such hearing is given to the king or chief as age, rank, military distinction or eloquence can secure; but it is rather their prestige as counsellors than their authority that tells. If a proposal displeases them, the people roar out their dissent; if they approve, they clash their spears. No form of approval can carry more honour than praise expressed by arms.

12

One can launch an accusation before the Council or bring a capital charge. The punishment varies to suit the crime. The traitor and deserter are hanged on trees, the coward, the shirker and the unnaturally vicious are drowned in miry swamps under a cover of wattled hurdles. The distinction in the punishments implies that deeds of violence should be paid for in the full glare of publicity, but that deeds of shame should be suppressed. Even for lighter offences the punishment varies. The man who is found guilty is fined so and so many horses or cattle. Part of the fine is paid to the King or State, part to the injured man or his relatives. In the same councils are elected the chiefs, who dispense justice through the country districts and villages. Each of them is attended by a hundred companions, drawn from the commons, both to advise him and to add weight to his decisions.

13

No business, public or private, is transacted except in arms. But it is the rule that no one shall take up his arms until the State has attested that he is likely to make good. When that time comes, one of the chiefs or the father or a kinsman equips the young warrior with shield and spear in the public council. This with the Germans is the equivalent of our *toga*—the first public distinction of youth. They cease to rank merely as members of the household and are now members of the state. Conspicuous ancestry or great services rendered by their fathers can win the rank of chief for boys still in their teens. They are attached to the other chiefs, who are more mature and approved, and no one blushes to be seen thus in the ranks of the companions. This order of companions has even its different grades, as determined by the leader, and there is intense rivalry among the companions for the first place by the chief, among the chiefs for the most numerous and enthusiastic companions. Dignity and power alike consist in being continually attended by a corps of chosen youths. This gives you consideration in peace-time and security in war. Nor is it only in a man's own nation that he can win name and fame by the superior number and quality of his companions, but in neighbouring states as well. Chiefs are courted by embassies and complimented by gifts, and they often virtually decide wars by the mere weight of their reputation.

14

On the field of battle it is a disgrace to the chief to be surpassed in valour by his companions, to the companions not to come up to the valour of their chief. As for leaving a battle alive after your chief has fallen, *that* means lifelong infamy and shame. To defend and protect him, to put down one's own acts of heroism to his credit—that is what they really mean by 'allegiance'. The chiefs fight for victory, the companions for their chief. Many noble youths, if the land of their birth is stagnating in a protracted peace, deliberately seek out other tribes, where some war is afoot. The Germans have no taste for peace; renown is easier won among perils, and you cannot maintain a large body of companions except by violence and war. The companions are prodigal in their demands on the generosity of their chiefs. It is always 'give me that war-horse' or 'give me that bloody and victorious spear'. As for meals with their plentiful, if homely, fare, they count simply as pay. Such open-handedness must have war and plunder to feed it. You will find it harder to persuade a German to plough the land and to await its annual produce with patience than to challenge a foe and earn the prize of wounds. He thinks it spiritless and slack to gain by sweat what he can buy with blood.

15

When not engaged in warfare, they spend some little time in hunting, but more in idling, abandoned to sleep and gluttony. All the heroes and grim warriors dawdle their time away, while the care of house, hearth and fields is left to the women, old men and weaklings of the family. The warriors themselves lose their edge. They are so strangely inconsistent. They love indolence, but they hate peace. It is usual for states to make voluntary and individual contributions of cattle or agricultural produce to the chiefs. These are accepted as a token of honour, but serve also to relieve essential needs. The chiefs take peculiar pleasure in gifts from neighbouring states, such as are sent not only by individuals, but by the community as well—choice horses, splendid arms, metal discs and collars; the practice of accepting money payments they have now learnt—from us.

16

It is a well-known fact that the peoples of Germany never live in cities, and will not even have their houses set close together. They live apart, dotted here and there, where spring, plain or grove has taken their fancy. Their villages are not laid out in Roman style, with buildings adjacent or interlocked. Every man leaves an open space round his house, perhaps as a precaution against the risk of fire, perhaps because they are such inexpert builders. They do not even make any use of little stone blocks or tiles; what serves their every purpose is ugly timber, both unimpressive and unattractive. They smear over some parts of their houses with an earth that is so pure and brilliant that it looks like painting or coloured mosaics. They have also the habit of hollowing out caves underground and heaping masses of refuse on the top. In these they can escape the winter's cold and store their produce. In such shelters they take the edge off the bitter frosts; and, should an invader come, he ravages the open country, but the secret and buried stores may pass altogether unnoticed or escape detection, simply because they have to be looked for.

17

The universal dress is the short cloak, fastened with a brooch or, failing that, a thorn. They pass whole days by the hearth fire wearing no garment but this. The richest are not distinguished, like the Persians and Sarmatians, by a long flowing robe, but by a tight one that shows the shape of every limb. They also wear the pelts of wild animals, the tribes near the Rhine without regard to appearance, the more distant peoples with some refinement of taste, for there is no other finery that they can buy. These latter peoples make careful choice of animal, then strip off the pelt and mottle it with patches of the spotted skins of the beasts that live in the outer ocean and the unknown sea. The dress of the women differs from that of the men in two respects only. The women often wear undergarments of linen, embroidered with purple, and, as the upper part does not extend to sleeves, forearms and upper arms are bare. Even the breast, where it comes nearest the shoulder, is exposed too.

18

For all that, marriage in Germany is austere, and there is no feature in their morality that deserves higher praise. They are almost unique among barbarians in being satisfied with one wife each. The exceptions, which are exceedingly rare, are of men who receive offers of many wives because of their rank; there is no question of sexual passion. The dowry is brought by husband to wife, not by wife to husband. Parents and kinsmen attend and approve of the gifts, gifts not chosen to please a woman's whim or gaily deck a young bride, but oxen, horse with reins, shield, spear and sword. For such gifts a man gets his wife, and she in her turn brings some present of arms to her husband. In this interchange of gifts they recognize the supreme bond, the holy mysteries, the presiding deities of marriage. A woman must not imagine herself free to neglect the manly virtues or immune from the hazards of war. That is why she is reminded, in the very ceremonies which bless her marriage at its outset, that she is coming to share a man's toils and dangers, that she is to be his partner in all his sufferings and adventures, whether in peace or war. That is the meaning of the team of oxen, of the horse ready for its rider, of the gift of arms. On these terms she must live her life and bear her children. She is receiving something that she must hand over unspoilt and treasured to her children, for her son's wives to receive in their turn and pass on to the grandchildren.

19

Thus it is that the German women live in a chastity that is impregnable, uncorrupted by the temptations of public shows or the excitements of banquets. Clandestine love-letters are unknown to men and women alike. Adultery in that populous nation is rare in the extreme, and punishment is summary and left to the husband. He shaves off his wife's hair, strips her in the presence of kinsmen, thrusts her from his house and flogs her through the whole village. They have, in fact, no mercy on a woman who prostitutes her chastity. Neither beauty, youth nor wealth can find the sinner a husband. No one in Germany finds vice amusing, or calls it 'up-to-date' to debauch and be debauched. It is still better with those states in which only virgins marry, and the hopes and prayers of a wife are settled once and for all. They take one husband, like the one body or life that they possess. No thought or desire must stray beyond him. They must not love the husband so much as the married state. To restrict the number of children or to put to death any born after the heir is considered criminal. Good morality is more effective in Germany than good laws in some places that we know.

20

The children grow up in every home, naked and dirty, to that strength of limb and size of body which excite our admiration. Every mother feeds her child at the breast and does not depute the task to maids and nurses. The master is not to be distinguished from the slave by any pampering in his upbringing. They grow up together among the same flocks and on the same ground, until maturity sets apart the free and the spirit of valour claims them as her own. The young men are slow to mate, and their powers, therefore, are never exhausted. The girls, too, are not hurried into marriage. As old and full-grown as the men, they match their mates in age and strength, and the children reproduce the might of their parents. The sons of sisters are as highly honoured by their uncles as by their own fathers. Some even go so far as to regard this tie of blood as peculiarly close and sacred, and, in taking hostages, insist on having them of this class; they think that this gives them a firmer grip on men's hearts and a wider hold on the family. However, a man's heirs and successors are his own children, and there is no such thing as a will; where there are no children, the next to succeed are, first, brothers, and then uncles, first on the father's, then on the mother's side. The larger a man's kin and the greater the number of his relations by marriage, the stronger is his influence when he is old. Childlessness in Germany is not a paying profession.

21

A man is bound to take up the feuds as well as the friendships of father or kinsman. But feuds do not continue unreconciled. Even homicide can be atoned for by a fixed number of cattle or sheep, and the satisfaction is received by the whole family. This is much to the advantage of the community, for private feuds are peculiarly dangerous side by side with liberty.

No nation abandons itself more completely to banqueting and entertainment than the German. It is accounted a sin to turn any man away from your door. The host welcomes his guest with the best meal that his means allow. When supplies run out, the host takes on a fresh rôle; he directs and escorts his guest to a new hostelry. The two go on, uninvited, to the nearest house. It makes no difference; they are welcomed just as warmly. No distinction is ever made between acquaintance and stranger as far as the right to hospitality is concerned. As the guest takes his leave, it is usual to let him have anything he asks for; the host, too, is no more shy in asking. They take delight in presents, but ask no credit for giving them and admit no obligation in receiving them. There is a pleasant courtesy in the relations between host and guest.

22

As soon as they rise from their sleep, which is often protracted well into the day, they wash in water that is usually warm; can one wonder, where winter holds such sway? After washing, they breakfast; each has his special place and his special table. Then they sally forth in arms to business or, as often as not, to banquets. Drinking bouts, lasting a day and night, are not considered in any way disgraceful. Such quarrels as inevitably arise over the cups are seldom settled by mere hard words, more often by blows and wounds. None the less, they often make banquets an occasion for discussing such serious affairs as the reconciliation of enemies, the forming of marriage alliances, the adoption of new chiefs, and even the choice of peace or war. At no other time, they feel, is the heart so open to frank suggestions or so quick to warm to a great appeal. The Germans are neither canny nor cunning, and take advantage of the occasion to unbosom themselves of their most secret thoughts; every soul is naked and exposed. The next day, comes reconsideration, and so due account is taken of both occasions. They debate at a time which cuts out pretence, they decide at a time that precludes mistake.

23

For drink they extract a juice from barley or grain, which is fermented to make something not unlike wine. The Germans who live nearest the Rhine can actually get wine in the market. Their food is plain—wild fruit, fresh game or curdled milk. They satisfy their hunger without any elaborate service or appetizers. But they show no corresponding self-control in drinking. You have only to indulge their intemperance by supplying all that they crave, and you will gain as easy a victory through their vices as through your own arms.

24

They have only one form of public show, which is the same wherever they foregather. Naked youths, trained to the sport, dance among swords and spears that are levelled at them. Practice begets skill, and skill grace, but they are not professionals or paid. However adventurous the play, their only reward is the pleasure they give the spectators. But they go in for dicing, if you can believe it, in all seriousness and in their sober hours, and are so recklessly keen about winning or losing that, when everything else is gone, they stake their personal liberty on the last decisive throw. The loser goes into slavery without complaint; younger or stronger he may be, but he suffers himself to be bound. Such is their perverse persistence, or, to use their own word, their honour. Slaves of this sort are sold and passed on, so that the winner may be clear of the shame that even he feels in his victory.

25

Slaves in general are not allotted, as we allot them, to special duties in the establishment. Each has control of his own house and home. The master imposes a fixed charge of grain, cattle or clothing, as he would on a tenant, and up to this point the slave will obey; but domestic tasks, as a whole, are performed by a man's wife and children. It is seldom that they flog a slave or punish him with imprisonment or forced labour; but they often put one to death, in no spirit of stern discipline, but in a fit of passion, as they might an enemy—only they have not to pay for it. Freedmen rank little higher than slaves; they have seldom any serious influence in the household, never in the State, excepting only in nations under the rule of kings. There they mount high above free men and nobles. With the rest the inferiority of freedmen is the hall-mark of liberty.

26

The practice of usury and compound interest is simply unknown. Ignorance here is a surer defence than any ban. Lands are taken into occupation, turn and turn about, by whole villages in proportion to the number of cultivators, and are then allotted in order of rank. The distribution is made easy by the vast extent of open land. They change their plough-lands yearly, and still there is ground to spare. The fact is that their soil is fertile and plentiful, but they refuse to give it the labour it deserves. They plant no orchards, fence off no meadows, water no gardens; the only levy on the earth is the corn crop. Hence it comes that they divide the year into fewer seasons than we do. Winter, spring and summer are familiar to them both as ideas and as names, but autumn is as unknown to them, as are the gifts she has to bring.

27

There is no pomp about their funerals. The one rule observed is that the bodies of famous men are burned with special kinds of wood. When they have heaped up the fire they do not throw robes or spices on the top; but only a man's arms, and sometimes his horse, too, are cast into the flames. The tomb is a raised mound of turf. They disdain to show honour by laboriously rearing high monuments of stone; they would only lie heavy on the dead.

Weeping and wailing are soon abandoned—sorrow and mourning not so soon. A woman may decently express her grief in public; a man should nurse his in his heart.

Such is the general account that we find given of the origin and customs of the Germans as a whole. I must now set forth the institutions and practices of the nations severally, so far as they are distinctive, and note the tribes that migrated into Gaul.

28

That the power of Gaul once exceeded that of Germany is recorded by that greatest of authorities, the deified Julius; and, in view of that, we may well believe that the Gauls in their time crossed into Germany. There was only a stream between, and how paltry an obstacle was that to stop any nation that grew strong enough from seizing and continuing to seize ever fresh lands, when they were no man's property and not yet partitioned between powerful kings! Thus, between the Hercynian forest and the rivers Rhine and Main, we find the Helvetii settled; beyond them, the Boii, both peoples of Gaul. The name of Bohemia still clings to the land and indicates its ancient history, even after its change of inhabitants. Whether the Aravisci came as immigrants to Pannonia from the German tribe of the Osi, or the Osi from the Aravisci into Germany, cannot be determined. Both speak the same language and have the same customs and character.

Furthermore, of old, when both banks of the Rhine were equally poor and equally free, they offered identical advantages and disadvantages. The Treviri and Nervii even go out of their way to claim German descent. Such a glorious origin, they feel, should clear them of any resemblance to the nerveless Gauls. The actual bank of the Rhine is held by peoples of undoubted German origin— the Vangiones, the Triboci and the Nemetes. Even the Ubii, for all that they have earned the rank of Roman colony and prefer to be called Agrippinenses, after Agrippina, their foundress, are not ashamed of their origin. They crossed the Rhine many years ago and, now that their loyalty to us is proved, they are stationed right on the river-bank, not to be under surveillance, but to keep the gate against intruders.

29

The most conspicuously courageous of all these peoples, the Batavi, hold little of the bank, but *do* hold the Rhine island. They were once a people of the Chatti, and on occasion of civil war migrated to their present homes— destined there to become a part of the Roman Empire. But the honour and distinction of their old alliance remain. They are not insulted by tribute or ground down by the tax-gatherer. Free from imposts and special levies, and reserved for battle, they are like weapons and armour, 'only to be used in war'. No less dutiful is the nation of the

Mattiaci, across the Rhine; for the greatness of Rome has spread the awe of her Empire even beyond the Rhine and the ancient frontiers. In geographical position they are on the German side, in heart and soul they are with us. They are similar to the Batavians in every way—except that soil and climate give a keener edge to their spirit.

I am inclined not to reckon among the people of Germany the cultivators of the *Agri decumates*, settled though they may be between Rhine and Danube. All the wastrels of Gaul, all the penniless adventurers seized on what was still no man's land. It was only later, when the frontier line of defence was drawn and the garrisons were moved forward, that they have become a sort of projection of the empire and a part of a province.

30

Beyond them dwell the Chatti, from the Hercynian forest onward, in a country less wide and marshy than the other states, which Germany stretches out to form. For the hills run on, and only thin out gradually, and the Hercynian forest, like a nurse with her infant cares, shows the Chatti on their way, and finally sets them down in the plain. This nation is distinguished by great physical hardiness, tautness of limb, savagery of expression and unusual mental vigour. They have plenty of judgment and acumen, as measured by the German standard. They pick the men to lead them, and proceed to obey them. They know how to keep their ranks, seize a chance, or delay an attack. They can map out the duties of the day or make sure the defences of the night. They reckon fortune a chance, but valour a certainty. They can also rise to an unusual achievement, usually reserved for Roman discipline: they place more dependence on the general than on the army. Their strength lies in their infantry, which, over and above its arms, has to bear the burden of entrenching tools and provisions. Other Germans may be seen going to battle, only the Chatti to war. It is but seldom that they engage in sallies or in broken fighting, such as really belong to cavalry, with its quick triumphs and its quick retreats. With infantry, speed is next door to cowardice, deliberate action approximates to courage.

31

A custom that in other German peoples is uncommon and depends on the enterprise of the individual has among the Chatti become a general rule—the letting the hair and beard grow long as soon as one has come of age, and only clearing the face of this covering, which has been vowed and pledged to valour, when one has slain an enemy. Over the bloodstained spoils they unbare the brow. 'Now at last,' they cry, 'we have paid the price of birth and shown ourselves worthy of country and parents.' The coward and the shirker remain still unkempt. The bravest also all wear an iron ring—which to the Chatti implies disgrace—

as a bond from which only the killing of an enemy can free them. Very many of the Chatti like this fashion and still signalize themselves by it even till their hair turns white—a mark for friend and foe alike. With such old warriors it always rests to begin the battle. They are always in the van and present a startling sight; even in peace they decline to soften the savagery of their expression. None of them has home, land or business of his own. To whatever host they choose to go, they get their keep from him, wasting the goods of others while despising their own, until old age drains their blood and incapacitates them for so exacting a form of heroism.

32

Next to the Chatti, along a Rhine that has now defined its channel and can serve as a boundary, live the Usipi and Tencteri. The Tencteri, while sharing in the general military glory, excel in skilful horsemanship. The infantry of the Chatti are not more famous than the cavalry of the Tencteri. That is their inherited tradition, which later ages continue to honour. The games of the children, the competitions of the young men, all take this same direction; even the old persist in it. Horses are handed down as part of the household with its protecting gods and the rights of the succession. They are inherited by a son, not necessarily, like the rest of the property, by the eldest, but by the one who is the keenest and ablest soldier.

33

Next to the Tencteri once came the Bructeri, but now
the Chamavi and Angrivarii are said to have taken their
place. The Bructeri were ousted and almost annihilated
by a league of neighbouring tribes. Perhaps they were
hated for their pride, or it may have been the lure of booty,
or else the gods were kind to Rome. We were even
gratified with the spectacle of a battle. Over 60,000
Germans fell, and not by Roman swords or javelins, but,
more splendid still, to gladden Roman eyes. Long, I
pray, may the Germans persist, if not in loving us, at least
in hating one another; for the imperial destiny drives hard,
and fortune has no longer any better gift for us than the
disunion of our foes.

34

The Angrivarii and Chamavi are shut in from behind
by the Dulgubnii, Chasuarii and other peoples of no
special note, whilst in the West they are succeeded by the
Frisii. The Frisii are called the 'greater' and the 'lesser', in
accordance with the actual strength of the two peoples.
Both tribes have the Rhine as their border right down to
Ocean, and their settlements also extend round vast lakes,
which have been sailed by Roman fleets. We have even
felt our way into Ocean by this route, and rumour has it
that there are pillars of Hercules beyond. Did Hercules
really go there, or is it only our habit of assigning any

conspicuous achievement anywhere to that famous name?
Drusus Germanicus was not deficient in the courage of
the explorer, but Ocean forbade further research into its
own secrets or those of Hercules. Since then no one has
tried to explore. It has been judged more pious and rever-
ent to believe in what the gods have done than to investigate it.

35

This is as far as the Germany we know extends to the
westward. To the north it comes back in a huge sweep.
The very first nation here is that of the Chauci. They
begin after the Frisians and hold a section of the coast, but
they also lie along the flanks of all those nations that I have
been describing, and finally curve back to meet the Chatti.
This huge stretch of country is not merely occupied, but
filled to overflowing by the Chauci. They are one of
the noblest peoples of Germany, and one that actually
prefers to maintain its greatness by righteous dealing.
Unvexed by greed or lawless ambition, they dwell in
quiet seclusion, never provoking a war, never robbing
or plundering their neighbours. It is conspicuous proof
of their valour and strength that their acknowledged
superiority does not rest on aggression. Yet every man
has arms ready to his hand, and, if occasion demands
it, they have vast reserves of men and horses. So, even
when they are at peace, their reputation does not fall.

36

On the flank of the Chauci and Chatti the Cherusci have been left free to enjoy a peace, too deep and over-ripe—a pleasant but perilous indulgence among powerful aggressors, where there is no true peace. When the strong hand decides, reasonableness and integrity have no meaning except as applied to the conqueror; and so the Cherusci, once the good and true, now hear themselves called the slovenly and slack. The luck of the victorious Chatti has come to rank as deep policy. In the fall of the Cherusci was involved the neighbouring tribe of the Fosi. They played second string to them in prosperity, but get an equal share of their adversity.

37

In the same bend of Germany, next to Ocean, dwell the Cimbri, a mighty name in history, though now but a tiny State. The traces of their ancient fame may still be seen far and wide, in vast encampments on both sides of the Rhine, which, by their huge girth, still supply a gauge of the mass and man-power of the nation and the historical truth of that great exodus. Rome was in her six hundred and fortieth year when the alarm of the Cimbrian arms was first heard, in the consulship of Caecilius Metellus and Papirius Carbo. Reckoning from that year to the second consulship of our Emperor Trajan, we get a total of just about two hundred and ten years. That is the time it is taking to conquer Germany. In the course of that long period much punishment has been given and taken by us. Neither from the Samnites nor from the Carthaginians, neither from Spain nor Gaul nor from the Parthians even, have we had more painful lessons. The freedom of Germany is a deadlier enemy than the despotism of Arsaces. After all, with what has the East to taunt us except the slaughter of Crassus? And after that it soon lost its own Pacorus and was humbled at the feet of Ventidius. But the Germans routed or captured Carbo, Cassius, Aurelius Scaurus, Servilius Caepio and Mallius Maximus, and robbed the Roman people, almost at one stroke, of five consular armies. From Caesar they stole Varus and his three legions. It was not without painful loss that C. Marius smote the Germans in Italy, that the deified Julius smote them in Gaul, that Drusus, Nero and Germanicus smote them in their own homes. Then the vast threats of Gaius Caesar ended in farce. After that ensued a peace, until the Germans took advantage of our dissensions and civil wars to storm the quarters of the legions and claim possession of Gaul. Driven back from these pretensions, they have in recent times supplied us with more triumphs than victories.

38

We must come now to speak of the Suebi, who do not, like the Chatti or Tencteri, constitute a single nation.

They actually occupy more than half Germany, and are divided into a number of distinct tribes under distinct names, though all generically are called Suebi. It is the special characteristic of this nation to comb the hair sideways and fasten it below with a knot. This distinguishes the Suebi from the rest of the Germans; this, among the Suebi, distinguishes the freeman from the slave. In other nations that are either related in some degree to the Suebi or indulge in the common habit of imitation the practice *does* exist, but is uncommon and confined to early manhood. But with the Suebi the bristling hair, even till it turns white, is twisted back and often knotted on the very crown of the head. The chiefs use an even more elaborate style. Such attention do they pay to their personal appearance—and yet in all innocence; it is not to make love or inspire it that they build their hair to such a terrifying height; all this elaborate make-up is to impress the foe they will meet in battle.

39

The oldest and noblest of the Suebi, so it is said, are the Semnones, and the justice of this claim is confirmed by a religious rite. At a set time all the peoples of this blood gather, in their embassies, in a wood hallowed by the auguries of their ancestors and the awe of ages. The sacrifice in public of a human victim marks the grisly opening of their savage ritual. In another way, too, reverence is paid to the grove. No one may enter it unless he is bound with a cord. By this he acknowledges his own inferiority and the power of the deity. Should he chance to fall, he must not get up on his feet again. He must roll out over the ground. All this complex of superstition reflects the belief that in that grove the nation had its birth, and that there dwells the god who rules over all, while the rest of the world is subject to his sway. Weight is lent to this belief by the prosperity of the Semnones. They dwell in a hundred country districts and, in virtue of their magnitude, count themselves chief of all the Suebi.

40

The Langobardi, by contrast, are distinguished by the fewness of their numbers. Ringed round as they are by many mighty peoples, they find safety, not in obsequiousness but in battle and its perils. After them come the Reudigni, Aviones, Anglii, Varini, Eudoses, Suarini and Nuitones behind their ramparts of rivers and woods. There is nothing particularly noteworthy about these people in detail, but they are distinguished by a common worship of Nerthus, or Mother Earth. They believe that she interests herself in human affairs and rides through their peoples. In an island of Ocean stands a sacred grove, and in the grove stands a car draped with a cloth which none but the priest may touch. The priest can feel the presence of the goddess in this holy of holies, and attends her, in deepest

reverence, as her car is drawn by kine. Then follow days
of rejoicing and merry-making in every place that she
honours with her advent and stay. No one goes to war,
no one takes up arms; every object of iron is locked away;
then, and then only, are peace and quiet known and prized,
until the goddess is again restored to her temple by the
priest, when she has had her fill of the society of men.
After that, the car, the cloth and, believe it if you will, the
goddess herself are washed clean in a secluded lake. This
service is performed by slaves who are immediately afterwards drowned in the lake. Thus mystery begets terror
and a pious reluctance to ask what that sight can be which
is allowed only to dying eyes.

41

This section of Suebian territory that I have been
describing juts out into the inner recesses of Germany.
Nearer to us, if we now follow the course of the Danube,
as we have been following that of the Rhine, come the
Hermunduri, our faithful allies. It is because they are our
allies that they are the only Germans who trade with us,
not only on the river-bank, but deep inside our lines, in the
brilliant colony that is the capital of Rhaetia. They come
over where they will, and without a guard. To other
nations we only show off our arms and our camps; to
them we expose our palaces and our country mansions—
and they do not covet them. In the territory of the Her-

munduri rises the river Elbe, once world-famous, now a mere name.

42

Next to the Hermunduri dwell the Naristi, followed by the Marcomanni and Quadi. The Marcomanni are conspicuous in renown and power; they won the very land they now hold by their bravery, when they drove out the Boii. Nor do the Naristi and Quadi fall below their high standard. These people form the front, so to speak, presented to us by Germany, where it is girt by the Danube. The Marcomanni and Quadi down to our own times retained kings of their own race, the noble line of Maroboduus and Tudrus, but now they submit to foreigners too. The might and power of the kings depend upon the authority of Rome. These kings occasionally receive our armed assistance, more often our financial, and it is equally effective.

43

The rear of the Marcommani and Quadi is shut in by the Marsigni, Cotini, Osi and Buri. Of these, the Marsigni and Buri, in language and mode of life, recall the Suebi. The Cotini and Osi are not Germans; that is proved by their languages, Gallic in the one case, Pannonian in the other, and also by the fact that they submit to paying tribute. Part of the tribute is levied by the Sarmatians, part by the Quadi, who regard them as men of foreign blood; the Cotini, more to their shame, have iron to mine. All these people are settled in country with little plain, but plenty of uplands, mountain peaks and high ground. Suebia, in fact, is parted down the middle by a range of mountains, and beyond that live a multitude of peoples, among whom the name of the Lugii is the widest spread, covering, as it does, a multitude of States. I need only give the names of the most powerful—the Harii, Helvecones, Manimi, Helisii and Naharvali. In the territory of the Naharvali one is shown a grove, hallowed from ancient times. The presiding priest dresses like a woman; the gods, translated into Latin, are Castor and Pollux. That expresses the character of the gods, but their name is Alci. There are no images, there is no trace of foreign cult, but they are certainly worshipped as young men and as brothers. As for the Harii, they are superior in strength to the other peoples I have just mentioned, and they pander to their savage instincts by choice of trickery and time. They black their shields and dye their bodies black and choose pitch dark nights for their battles. The terrifying shadow of such a fiendish army inspires a mortal panic, for no enemy can stand so strange and devilish a sight. Defeat in battle always begins with the eyes.

Passing the Lugii, we find the Gothones under the rule of kings. It is a slightly stricter rule than in the rest of the German peoples, but yet does not pass the bounds of freedom. Then, immediately bordering on the ocean, are the Rugii and Lemovii. All these peoples are distinguished by round shields, short swords and submission to regal authority.

44

The states of the Suiones that follow along the shore of Ocean are strong not only in arms and men but also in their fleets. The shape of their ships differs from the normal in having a prow at both ends, which is always ready to be put in to shore. They do not rig sails or fasten their oars in banks at the sides. Their oarage is loose, as one finds it on some rivers, and can be shifted, as need requires, from side to side. Wealth, too, is held in high honour, and that is why they obey one ruler, with no restrictions on his authority and with no mere casual claim to obedience. Arms are not, as in the rest of Germany, allowed to all and sundry, but are kept under custody, and the custodian is a slave. There are two reasons for this: the ocean makes any sudden invasion impossible, and men with arms in their hands easily get into mischief, if not fighting. As for putting no noble or freeman, or even freedman, in charge of the arms—that is part of royal policy.

45

Passing the Suiones, we find yet another sea that is sluggish and almost stagnant. The reason why this sea is believed to be the boundary that girds the earth is because

the last radiance of the setting sun lasts here till dawn, with
a brilliance that dims the stars. Rumour adds that you can
hear the sound he makes as he leaves the waves and can see
the shape of his horses and the rays on his head. At this
point our real knowledge of the world ends. However,
turning to the right shore of the Suebian sea, we find it
washing the territories of the Aestii, who have the
religion and general customs of the Suebi, but a language
approximating to the British. They worship the Mother
of the gods. They wear, as emblem of this cult, the masks
of boars, which stand them in stead of armour or human
protection and ensure the safety of the worshipper even
among his enemies. They seldom use weapons of iron,
but cudgels often. They cultivate grain and other crops
with a patience quite unusual among lazy Germans. Nor
do they omit to ransack the sea; they are the only people
to collect the amber—*glaesum* is their own word for it—in
the shallows or even on the beach. Like true barbarians,
they have never asked or discovered what it is or how it is
produced. For a long time, indeed, it lay unheeded like
any other jetsam, until Roman luxury made its reputation.
They have no use for it themselves. They gather it crude,
pass it on unworked and are astounded at the price it
fetches. Amber, however, is certainly a gum of trees, as
you may see from the fact that creeping and even winged
creatures are often seen shining in it. They got caught in
the sticky liquid, and were imprisoned as it hardened. I
imagine that in the islands and lands of the West, just as in

the secret chambers of the East, where the trees sweat frankincense and balm, there must be woods and groves of unusual fertility. Their gums, drawn out by the rays of their near neighbour, the sun, flow in liquid state into the sea and are finally washed by violent storms on to the shores opposite. If you care to test the properties of amber by applying fire to it, you will find that it lights like a torch and gives off a thick and heavily scented flame; it then cools into a sticky solid like pitch or resin.

Continuous with the Suiones are the nations of the Sitones. They resemble them in all respects but one—woman is the ruling sex. That is the measure of their decline, I will not say below freedom, but even below decent slavery.

46

Here Suebia ends. I cannot make up my mind whether to assign the tribes of the Peucini, Venedi and Fenni to Germany or Sarmatia. The Peucini, however, who are sometimes called the Bastarnae, in language, social habits, mode of settlement and dwelling are like Germans. They are a squalid and slovenly people; the features of their nobles get something of the Sarmatian ugliness from inter-marriage. The Venedi have borrowed largely from Sarmatian ways; their plundering forays take them over all that wooded and mountainous country that rises between the Peucini and the Fenni. Nevertheless they are to be classed as Germans, for they have settled houses, carry shields, and are fond of travelling—and travelling fast—on foot, in all these respects differing from the Sarmatians, who live in waggons or on horseback. The Fenni are astonishingly wild and horribly poor. They have no arms, no horses, no homes. They eat grass, dress in skins, and sleep on the ground. Their only hope is in their arrows, which, for lack of iron, they tip with bone. The same hunt provides food for men and women alike; for the women go everywhere with the men and claim a share in securing the prey. The only way they can protect their babies against wild beasts or foul weather is to hide them under a makeshift network of branches. This is the hovel to which the young men come back, this is where the old must lie. Yet they count their lot happier than that of others who groan over field labour, sweat over house-building, or hazard their own or other men's fortunes in the wild lottery of hope and fear. They care for nobody, man or god, and have gained the ultimate release: they have nothing to pray for. What comes after them is the stuff of fables—Hellusii and Oxiones with the faces and features of men, but the bodies and limbs of animals. On such unverifiable stories I will express no opinion.

NOTES ON THE AGRICOLA

I

Manuscripts and Manuscript Readings

The extant manuscripts of the *Agricola* are very few:

(1) and (2) Vatican, late 15th century.

(3) Toledo Chapter Library, late 15th century.

(4) Private library of Count Balleani at Iesi, near Ancona, a parchment of the 10th century, the ultimate source of (1) to (3), but not free from blemishes that go back to its origin. This manuscript was only recognized for what it is in September, 1902.

The text followed in this book is, in the main, that of Anderson (Furneaux, 2nd edition, Oxford Press, 1922). A few notes are added, where this rule is broken or where some special difficulty calls for comment.

Chapter 9. I retain 'tristitiam et adrogantiam et avaritiam exuerat', placed by Anderson in square brackets. There is no fatal objection to the words, and 'exuerat' is well in line with 'persona' just above.

Chapter 15. 'Felicibus' after 'plus impetus'—omitted in the Vatican manuscripts—is a very good illustration of the superiority of the Iesi tradition.

Chapter 19. 'Luere pretio', Iesi, retained by Anderson. Here I prefer 'ludere' of the Vatican MSS., which seems to yield a much better sense: After 'emere ultro frumentum' what precisely does 'luere pretio', 'make amends by the price', mean?

Chapter 24. I retain 'nave prima' with the MSS. and Anderson (doubtfully), and translate 'prima' as neuter plural; 'prima', ablative, 'in the first ship', is very poor sense.

Chapter 26. 'Nonanis', Iesi, Anderson. The Vatican MSS. read 'Romanis'. Another clear case of the superiority of Iesi.

Chapter 28. 'Remigante', MSS., printed by Anderson, but with an obelus; it gives no real sense. The sense required is 'while one complied with their wishes'. 'Morigerante' gives just this sense, and is preferable as an emendation to others already proposed, such as 'remigante' or 'renavigante'.

Chapter 30. Against the MSS. and Anderson, I accept the transposition, approved by most editors, of 'atque omne ignotum pro magnifico est' from after 'patet' to after 'defendit' above. The sense seems to gain very greatly by the change.

Chapter 31. 'Laturi', MSS., cannot be construed. 'Bellaturi' (Anderson after Koch) at least makes sense.

Chapter 33. Anderson, following Nipperdey, alters 'opera nostra' to 'opera vestra'—against the MSS. I can see no justification for the change. All through the passage Agricola is talking in balanced phrases of his soldiers and himself.

Chapter 43. 'Nobis nihil comperti adfirmare ausim', MSS.; 'I can only say that we have no certain evidence'. There is no need to insert 'ut' after 'comperti'; 'we have no evidence sufficient to justify a positive assertion'.

Chapter 44. The MSS. read 'quarto' and 'Prisco': 'sexto' and 'Priscino' are needed to be correct.

Chapter 45. Anderson inserts 'foedavit' to give a government to 'visus' (MSS.). But the Iesi and other MSS. have in margin 'Mauricum Rusticumque divisimus'. Like Anderson's suggestion, this seems to be an attempt to cure a sick passage. But I do not understand why the idea of the senate parting two brothers—sending one to death, the other to exile—should be thought 'unsuitable and insipid . . . in this context'.

Chapter 46. Anderson, following Haupt, reads 'obruit', present; but 'obruet', future, of the MSS. gives a good sense.

II
Notes on Certain Passages in Agricola

Chapter 4. The Romans from of old distrusted philosophy as an enemy of the active life. In 155 B.C. the Senate ordered all Greek philosophers to leave Rome. Under the Empire, philosophy was sometimes a cover for opposition to Government, and was resented as such. Domitian expelled philosophers from Rome in A.D. 93, possibly also earlier in A.D. 88–89.

Chapter 5. 'Titulus tribunatus' should mean that Agricola, while 'tribunus militum' in rank, was not assigned to any special legion. Anderson renders 'titulus' as 'distinction'—partly missing the meaning, as I think. An unassigned tribune could obviously be more easily spared.

Chapter 6. When elected to the quaestorship, a man drew his particular post by lot. It might either be in Rome or in the provinces.

The daughter 'strengthened' Agricola's position, because special privileges were allotted to the fathers of children. Agricola probably was enabled to hold the praetorship one year before the usual age (30).

The 'iurisdictio', which had been the main function of praetors under the Republic, belonged still to a few, notably to the 'praetor urbanus' and 'praetor peregrinus'. The task of celebrating the public games had been exclusively assigned to the praetors by Augustus.

After the Great Fire of Rome, A.D. 64, Nero had pillaged temples throughout the Empire. Private individuals, or even public officials like Vitellius as 'Commissioner of temples and public buildings', had followed the bad example. Agricola, acting as a special Commissioner, helped to recover all that could be recovered. The major depredations of Nero were past hope of recovery.

Chapter 9. The 'colleagues', if the word is used strictly, can only be the governors of neighbouring provinces, and that may be the meaning. But, as attention is concentrated on the internal affairs of Aquitania, 'colleagues' may be used loosely to include the senatorial 'legati' who, strictly speaking, were subordinates of Agricola. The procurators were the financial agents of the Emperor.

Chapter 10. The guesses at the shape of Britain cannot be considered happy.

The 'flumina' can be translated as 'currents'. But why not 'rivers'? The deep encroachments of the sea among the mountains could clearly be so described.

Chapter 11. The Celtic invaders of Britain came in at least three waves:

(a) Goidelic Celts—long before 400 B.C.
(b) Brythonic Celts—c. 400 B.C. and on
(c) Belgae from Gaul in mass shortly after 50 B.C.

From the Goidelic Celts come Gaelic, Irish and Manx; from the Brythonic, Welsh, Cornish and Breton.

The Gauls, when attacked by Caesar, were still a vigorous and war-like people. But the tide had already turned; they were no longer moving East across the Rhine, but the German tribes were pressing Westward against them. They soon settled down to Roman rule. It is curious that Tacitus should scoff at them for doing so.

Chapter 12. Quite a number of British kings are known from native coins—Cunobelinus (Cymbeline), Commius, Tincommius, Tasciovanus, Verica, etc.

Tacitus is imagining a disk-like earth, though its spherical shape was already known. The sun is thought to pass below the earth, and the flat edges of earth are not high enough to cast shadows to the sky.

Julius Caesar dedicated a necklace of British pearls in the temple of Venus Genetrix in Rome. It is curious that Tacitus says nothing of the oysters, which, especially at Rutupiae (Richborough), were famous.

Chapter 14. The 'colony' was Camulodunum (Colchester)—founded under Ostorius Scapula—containing a temple of Claudius.

Cp. the famous incription of Chichester, mentioning a 'Ti. Claudius Cogidubnus, king, legate of Augustus', c. A.D. 75–80.

Chapter 15. The Germans who 'threw off the yoke' were the Cherusci under Arminius, who destroyed Varus and his legions in A.D. 9. The river is, of course, the Rhine.

Chapter 18. *See back*, Chapters 14–16.

Chapter 19. The proceedings of the Roman profiteers (who might include any official from the governor downwards) are somewhat obscure, though certainly nefarious. The levy of corn was, it seems, made by the governor and was in addition to the tribute, paid in money. There were two main abuses:

(1) Where corn was scarce, the natives had to buy from Rome the corn they were to deliver back. Actually it stayed in the public granaries all the time.

(2) Where corn was plentiful, the natives were told to deliver it, at great inconvenience, to distant places. They presumably paid to be given easier terms.

But it seems to me possible that the abuse was even worse—that, first, corn was requisitioned irregularly, then requisitioned in due form and sold back to the natives at absurd (high) prices, finally paid for by the Government again at farcical (low) prices. Roman extortion when bad was very thorough.

Chapter 20. The 'strong points' and 'forts' were mainly for the defence of the new Roman gains against their unconquered countrymen.

Chapter 21. Anderson seems to make a difficulty here, when he denies that the meaning is 'expressed a preference for British abilities over Gallic industry'. It need *not* imply that British abilities were not cultivated—only that they were (in Agricola's view) superior to the Gallic, and so able to catch up the start that the Gauls had had.

Chapter 22. For Agricola's forts, *see* Anderson's introduction S, ii–iii.

Chapter 23. The line of Clyde and Forth is a natural line of defence. The *virtus exercituum et Romani nominis gloria* is perhaps only a euphemism for the ambition of Agricola.

North of the Clyde and Forth no natural frontier can be found. The whole island would need to be conquered and held.

Chapter 28. The Usipi (Usipetes) dwelt on the Rhine between the Lippe and Yssel. If Mommsen's view that they were only annexed by Domitian in A.D. 83 were correct, this sixth year of Agricola would be A.D. 83, his seventh and last A.D. 84, his first therefore A.D. 78. But really it is only a guess, and Tacitus, in clear terms, marks A.D. 77 as Agricola's first year.

There is no indication of the point from which the Usipi started or the direction in which they sailed. Perhaps the more likely view is that they set out from the coast of Cumberland and sailed north and east round Cape Wrath, to end up on the coasts of Holland and North Germany.

This chapter represents the high-water mark of Tacitean incoherence. The 'bank' at the end is the west (Gallic) bank of the Rhine.

Chapter 29. The modern name, 'Grampian', is derived from a misreading of the passage.

The 'fresh and green old age' is quoted from Virgil's description of Charon in Aeneid, VI. v. 304.

Chapter 31. Cohorts of Britons served in Germany, Pannonia and elsewhere. The daughters of Boudicca had been seduced by Roman officers.

It was not the Brigantes under their queen, Cartismandua, but

the Iceni, under Boudicca, who performed these exploits, as
Tacitus knew (*see* Chapter 16). Perhaps Tacitus deliberately puts
into the mouth of Calgacus what might seem a natural error.
The Brigantes were far nearer to him and more powerful than
the Iceni.

Cartismandua actually surrendered the patriot, Caratacus, to
the Romans, and sought Roman aid against her own rebel
subjects.

Chapter 32. *See above*, Chapter 28.

Probably *not* 'here (on our side) is a general and an army' (so
Anderson). Calgacus seems not to be contrasting patriots with
Romans, but the front of the Romans with their rear.

Chapter 33. It would have been natural here to speak of the 'valour
and auspices', not of the Roman Empire, but of the Roman
Emperor, Domitian. Could Agricola really have omitted to do
so? We can understand how Tacitus, in reporting, left out a
name that he hated.

Chapter 34. See Chapter 26 for the night-attack.

'Fifty years', a round figure, is well off the mark. The number
is actually forty-one, A.D. 43–83.

Chapter 35. The wise and economical policy of sparing the legionaries, whose recruitment and training were expensive, and using
instead the auxiliaries, who were cheaper and easier to get, is very
curiously described as 'ingens victoriae decus'—a vast enhance-
ment of the victory.

Chapter 39. Domitian triumphed over the Chatti in A.D. 83.
Frontinus reports serious gains on the German frontier, and
modern archaeology has confirmed his words. Tacitus is simply
reporting malicious gossip. No doubt there was often an element
of 'faking' in the actual make-up of even the most authentic
triumph.

The Emperor was 'imperator' *par excellence,* and, from that,
comes the name 'Emperor'. All victories were put down to his

credit. When first proclaimed Emperor, he assumed the title 'imp(erator)', and often bore it, as a *praenomen*, at the head of his title. Any victory on the large scale might bring to him, through his legate, a fresh salutation as 'imperator'. These victories were recorded by the word 'imp.', with number, at the end of the title.

Chapter 40. The will of the Emperor was often made effective by 'senatus consulta', decrees of the senate, proposed by the Emperor and duly ratified by the obedient senators.

Chapter 41. The fighting went on from A.D. 85 to c. A.D. 93. The chief enemies were the Daci, the Quadi and the Sarmatian Iazyges. One of the worst disasters was the loss of Cornelius Fuscus, the praetorian prefect, with his army in A.D. 86 in the Dobrudja. 'Ripa' here is the bank of the Danube.

Chapter 42. Asia and Africa, both under proconsuls, were two of the crowning prizes of the senatorial career. Normally the lot decided between the two senior ex-consuls, who had not yet held either. The year will have been A.D. 91 or, perhaps better, 92. C. Vettulenus Civica Cerialis was put to death, while governor of Asia, c. A.D. 90.

Chapter 43. 'Aliud agens populus', the populace 'doing something else'—so 'bent on other (its own) affairs' or just 'indifferent'.

The meaning depends on the reading adopted. But, in any case, Tacitus, more or less clearly, hints at poisoning, while admitting that it could not be proved. In Chapter 44, 'festinatae mortis', 'premature death', seems to imply the poisoning as a fact.

The whole treatment of the subject does little credit to Tacitus.

It was a common practice to leave part of an inheritance to the Emperor away from the family, in order to secure the rest to them. Naturally it flourished in inverse proportion to the virtue of the Emperor. But good emperors also received legacies. Tacitus again is rather malicious.

Chapter 44. Agricola was born June 13th, A.D. 40, and died August 23rd, A.D. 93.

Trajan distinguished himself in A.D. 89 by helping to suppress the revolt of Saturninus. Adopted by Nerva in September, A.D. 97, he succeeded him on his death in January, A.D. 98. That his advancement should have been hopefully prophesied is quite credible, though not recorded elsewhere.

Chapter 45. The 'reign of terror' seems to have begun about A.D. 93. Among the noble ladies exiled were Arria, widow of Thrasea Paetus, and her daughter, Fannia, wife of Helvidius Priscus. The informers of Domitian (see Index of Names) were let loose, victims were brought to trial before the Senate, and the Senate sentenced them to exile or death.

Domitian was of a rubicund complexion, which made it impossible for him to 'turn red'. Domitian did not, according to Tacitus's caustic epigram, need to *do* anything. He simply retained his shameless red, while all decent men turned pale—and were betrayed by the contrast.

Agricola, dying what looked like a natural death, made it appear that Domitian had no share in it, and 'made the Emperor a present of innocence'. This is hardly to be reconciled completely with the hints about poisoning.

Tacitus was absent from Rome, *c.* A.D. 90–92, in some provincial appointment. It is characteristic of his method that he omits to tell us what it was.

NOTES ON THE GERMANIA

I

Manuscripts and Readings

This section, like the corresponding section in the *Agricola*, is intended for Latin scholars, and may be skipped by the general reader.

Unlike the *Agricola*, the *Germania* is known in a fair number of manuscripts—twenty-nine in all (in the Vatican, Leiden, Naples, etc.). The general opinion is that all are derived from one archetype, which survives only in a few leaves in the Codex Iesi (10th century—*see* notes on *Agricola*, above), but that the derivation is indirect, through a copy made in the 15th century. Professor R. P. Robinson of Connecticut has recently (1935) argued in favour of a distinct tradition, represented by three MSS. (Vienna, Munich, Hummelianus).

The text followed in this book is, in the main, that of Anderson (Furneaux, 2nd edition, Oxford Press). A few notes are added, when this rule is broken or where some special difficulty calls for comment.

Chapter 2. The emendation 'aversus' for 'adversus' has its attractions, but there is no sufficient reason for change. 'Adversus' = 'hostile' gives a good sense.

Chapter 13. I retain, with Anderson, the 'ceteris robustioribus' of the manuscripts. Anderson, however, suspects a later corruption. I avoid his difficulty by a different translation.

Chapter 15. I read, with Anderson (after Meiser), 'magnifica' instead of 'magna' (MSS.), but without conviction that the latter reading is not possible.

Chapter 21. 'Victus inter hospitis comis' is bracketed as a later addition by Anderson, following most editors. I retain it with some hesitation, because of its manuscript authority.

Chapter 28. I retain 'Germanicorum natione' after 'Osis' against Anderson and other editors. The words are in the manuscripts and can be construed.

Chapter 30. 'Peditum' is not in the manuscripts, but its insertion (Anderson, following Bährens) seems absolutely necessary.

Chapter 38. The last sentence 'Neque . . . ornantur' reads very badly, though the general sense is clear. Something is wrong. I do not find that it helps much to bracket 'ut' after 'compti' (so Anderson, following Halm). Lachmann's 'comptius' seems preferable. But the corruption surely lies deeper; 'neque enim ut ament amenturve' demands an explicit contrast to follow, and that contrast is not there.

Chapter 43. 'Iugumque' of the MSS. is bracketed by Anderson (following Acidalius). I retain it with some hesitation.

II

Notes on Certain Passages in the Germania

Chapter 1. The war is taken to be the campaign of Tiberius in A.D. 5 by land and sea. If this is right, 'nuper'—'recently'—is a very loose phrase. I suspect that later wars, not precisely recorded, may be in question.

Chapter 2. 'Nostro' in 'orbe nostro' means 'Roman', as often. Thus 'mare nostrum' is the Mediterranean.

The words 'eaque vera et antiqua nomina' are usually taken to be dependent on 'adfirmant' ('esse' supplied). A better meaning results if they are taken as a direct statement ('sunt' supplied). The names *are* old and genuine; the question is whether they are rightly connected with sons of Mannus.

The rendering of this famous passage, given in the text, is almost certainly correct. It has been defended with a great array of learning by Norden. The alternative version, 'that all were first called Germans by the victor to inspire terror', is, grammatically, easier, for 'a victore' and 'a se ipsis' will then be used in exactly the same sense, not, as in our rendering, with a shift of meaning. But the sense is poor—the Tungri (Germani), to frighten the Gauls, said that all the people across the Rhine were Germans too. 'Ob metum' *can* mean 'to inspire fear', but the other meaning, 'because of fear felt', is more usual.

Chapter 3. The transition from songs in praise of heroes to the wordless chant is rather awkward and surprising, but it is there. 'Baritus' (or 'barritus') is almost certainly the correct form; it means 'roar' (of an elephant, for example). 'Barditus' ('shield-song'?) has better manuscript authority, but can hardly be correct. Ammianus Marcellinus (16.12.43) has the form 'barritus'.

Chapter 4. The claim to special purity of race had been made before Tacitus for Egyptians and Scythians. Tacitus can never have dreamed of the terrible abuses which would grow out of his simple statement.

Chapter 5. Finds of precious metals in Germany are numerous enough to show that we must not take Tacitus too seriously here.

The 'pecunia vetus' was the denarius of the Republic, about 10*d*. in value. The 'bigati' had as reverse type Diana or Victory in a two-horse chariot ('biga'). The 'serrati' had notches in their edges, intended to show that the metal was pure. The two classes seem to be used, with some little inaccuracy, to denote the earlier Roman silver in general.

Chapter 6. Tacitus's account of German arms and clothing is strongly corroborated by the evidence of ancient coins, ancient statuettes and reliefs.

Tacitus's account of the 'centeni' is probably correct. The argument that the 'name and distinction' ought to belong to the cavalry rather than to the foot is beside the point. Tacitus is talking for the moment of the élite of the infantry.

Chapter 7. The account of German kingship applies mainly to the West Germans. In the East kings had more power (cp. Chapters 42, 43, 44).

Chapter 8. Drusilla, sister of Caligula, Claudia, infant daughter of Nero and Poppaea, and Poppaea herself had been consecrated as goddesses ('divae'). Tacitus seems to have accepted the consecration of men as a State necessity. He normally gives the title of 'divus' to Emperors who had been consecrated.

Chapter 9. Mercury is the German Wodan (Odin), Hercules is Donnar (Thor), Mars is Tiu.

Tacitus thinks that the goddess worshipped was the Egyptian Isis, not a German goddess identified with her. The galley suggests advent by sea; Isis was worshipped as goddess of the sea, and a spring festival, 'the release of ships', was celebrated in her honour, when the winter storms were past.

Chapter 11. There is no difficulty about Tacitus's 'principes', if we remember that they were simply men prominent by wealth or birth—not magistrates, but capable of being elected to magisterial posts.

Chapter 12. Matthew Arnold's lines (in 'Balder Dead') come to mind:

'Cowards, who were in sloughs interred alive;
And round them still the wattled hurdles hung,
Wherewith they stamped them down, and trod them deep
To hide their shameful memory from men'.

Victims of this punishment have been found in the North-West of Germany.

Again the 'centeni' (hundred) occur in a new context, and again the objections raised are inconclusive.

Chapter 13. Tacitus, I take it, definitely assigns the rank of 'chief' to his chosen youths. They do not at once take a prominent position, but are attached to the rest of the chiefs, who are of firmer age and better tried, and they are not in the least ashamed to be their 'companions'. He then goes on to use 'chief' in a restricted sense, as the head of companions. If this is right, the youths were 'principes' in contrast to the general mass of the population, but 'comites' to their own 'chief' ('princeps' in the narrower sense).

The alternative rendering, 'secure the approval of a chief', is barely possible Latin. It also makes nonsense of 'ceteris' following.

Anderson, I think, takes much the view that I do, but he expresses himself so cautiously that one is not quite sure. He also says that 'robustioribus' would be a 'ridiculous description of a man in the position of "princeps" '. But why?

Tacitus writes of the 'chiefs' and their 'companions' with obvious relish and appreciation.

Chapter 17. Tacitus's account of German dress is borne out wherever a detail can be checked by ancient reliefs and coins.

Chapter 18. The second sentence is very awkwardly expressed. As it reads, it would almost seem as if the 'libido' were in the women, not in the men—certainly not what Tacitus meant. Some phrase like 'take several wives' must be deduced out of 'ambiuntur'.

Chapter 19. 'Publicatae pudicitiae': Tacitus is thinking primarily of the adulteress, but the phrase applies to any kind of female unchastity.

Chapter 20. The childless old man and woman ('orbus', 'orba') and their courtiers ('captatores'), who were after their money, were a joke and a scandal at Rome in the early Empire. Calvia Crispinilla, a disreputable old noblewoman at Nero's court, survived his fall and enjoyed great influence from her wealth and childlessness.

Chapter 24. This is the 'sword dance', not unknown even to-day.

Chapter 25. Tacitus's account of German slavery is scanty and inaccurate.

'Nisi quod impune est'—'except that he has not to pay for it'—
a cruel phrase, but Tacitus's own.

Tacitus takes a rather malicious pleasure in emphasizing the
powerlessness of freedmen in Germany. In Rome, freedmen,
engaging freely in daring speculations, often made vast fortunes.
In the service of the Emperor, especially as heads of bureaux
(Finance, Correspondence), they might have serious political
influence. Domitian, Tacitus's '*bête noire*', had his own con-
fidential freedmen.

Chapter 26. Anderson denies that 'in usuras extendere' can mean 'to
increase by compound interest' and regards it as a vaguer
expansion of 'faenus agitare'.

Surely 'faenus agitare' means 'to take interest (simple)' and
'in usuras extendere' 'to extend (simple) into compound
interest'.

In the next sentence what is observed is the principle of 'no
usury'. It is safer for usury to be unknown than for it to be
forbidden.

Chapter 29. The 'Agri Decumates', in the territory between Rhine,
Main and Danube, were included in the empire by Vespasian and
his successors (*c*. A.D. 73–95). The name 'Decumates' is pre-
Roman. It does not mean 'tithe lands': it may be 'lands of ten
(cantons?)'.

Chapter 31. A confused chapter, but not necessarily spoilt by corruption. The young Chattan warrior lets his hair grow ('squalor')
and only shaves when he has killed his man. Only the coward
and shirker remain 'squalid'. (But what happens in peace-
time?)

The iron ring, worn as a sign of servitude, is also something
that can be discarded after victory. (An awkward interruption of
the discussion of 'squalor'.)

Many Chattans actually prefer to remain 'squalidi' ('hic
placet habitus'), go like this into battle and continue so till their

hair turns white. (This 'squalor' of the hero is quite different from that of the young. Yet Tacitus hardly gives a sign that he realized this.)

There is nothing really incredible in anything that Tacitus reports, but if he is correct in his statements he might have worked them up into a much more convincing picture.

Chapter 33. This tragedy of the Bructeri may have occurred in A.D. 98. Perhaps as a sequel to it a Roman general, Vestricius Spurinna, placed a king of the Bructeri on his throne. The Bructeri were certainly not so completely destroyed as Tacitus here says.

The Roman army of Lower Germany was apparently looking on at the battle. This gives point to Tacitus's somewhat tasteless phrase about the 'delight of Roman eyes'. It was like a great gladiatorial show.

The meaning of the last four lines has been much disputed. 'Urgentibus imperii fatis' certainly means almost exactly the same as 'urgentibus imperium fatis'—'while the fates of the empire press (or "drive") it on'. But is the tone serious and no more? Or mildly anxious? Or definitely pessimistic? Pessimistic, I am sure. Tacitus has *not* an open mind about the future of the Empire. The strain is growing too great, the burden too heavy. If he does not despair, it is because fate has still one precious gift to help Rome—the dissension of her foes.

Chapter 34. Drusus Germanicus is generally taken to be Nero Drusus who died in 9 B.C. If that is so, how can Tacitus write 'mox nemo temptavit', forgetting the exploits of Tiberius in A.D. 5, and of Germanicus in A.D. 15–16? The difficulty is perhaps unavoidable. It would be avoided if we took Drusus Germanicus to be our Germanicus and the reference to be only to his expedition. But the expeditions of Germanicus seem to have been purely military in purpose.

Chapter 35. The Chauci were won over by Nero Drusus in 12 B.C.

In A.D. 28 they joined in the Frisian revolt. They were on the side of Civilis, A.D. 69–70. Tacitus's high praise is not fully borne out by other authorities. Part, at any rate, of the people lived in poverty on the coast, and tried to improve its conditions by piracy, which led it into trouble with Rome in A.D. 41 and 47.

Chapter 36. Arminius died in A.D. 21. The Cherusci received a king from Rome in A.D. 47. In A.D. 85 their king, Chariomerus, driven out by the Chatti, obtained financial help, but no more, from Domitian.

Chapter 37. For the detail of the German wars, *see* Introduction, S. 10. The critical phrase is 'tam diu Germania vincitur'. Rome was not accustomed to this type of resistance. The reader is helped to draw his own conclusions from the closing words of the chapter—'triumphs perhaps, hardly true victories'.

The Samnites contested with Rome the chief military power in Italy in three great wars, lasting from 343 to 290 B.C. The bitterest blow to Rome was the defeat and capitulation at the Caudine Forks, 321 B.C. The Carthaginians also fought three great wars against Rome—the First Punic War, 264–241 B.C., the Second (the Hannibalic), 218–202 B.C., the Third, ending in the destruction of Carthage, 149–146 B.C. In the First war Rome lost a consular army (Regulus) in Africa and fleet after fleet in storms and defeats at sea. In the Second, Hannibal routed great Roman armies at the Trebia, Lake Trasimene and Cannae, wandered over Italy at will for half a generation, and at one moment threatened the very existence of Rome.

The conquest of Spain began in the Second Punic War, and was only rounded off under Augustus. The Lusitanians under Viriathus, c. 154 B.C. onwards, and the little town of Numantia, c. 139–133 B.C., caused Rome painful losses.

M. Crassus, the triumvir, invaded Parthia, without just reason, but was defeated and killed at Carrhae in Mesopotamia in 53 B.C., and Roman eagles were lost. Later, the Parthians took the offensive under Pacorus, son of their king, Orodes. But he was defeated and slain at Mt. Gindarus in Syria, 38 B.C., by P. Ventidius Bassus, an able but low-born lieutenant of Mark Antony.

Of course, Augustus is meant here by 'Caesar'. But the use is almost unexampled.

Drusus is our Nero Drusus, Germanicus our Germanicus; but what prompted Tacitus in this passage to call Tiberius 'Nero'?

The unusual descriptions of both Augustus and Tiberius must have been deliberately chosen by Tacitus. But it is hard to see why he should try to increase impressiveness by this means.

Chapter 38. The knots of the Suebi can be excellently illustrated from the ancient monuments.

Chapter 39. The number 'one hundred' is very high for the one tribe of the Semnones. Perhaps it should include the tribes that shared in this festival. Here, again, it has been suspected that Tacitus has misinterpreted 'hundred' = 'local district'.

Chapter 41. The 'colonia' can be none other than Augusta Vindelicum (Augsburg). But 'colony' is a misnomer. The town was founded by Nero Drusus in 15 B.C., and made a 'municipium' under Hadrian.

Chapter 42. As Maroboduus was certainly the great king of the Marcomanni, Tuder (or Tudrus) must have been the great king of the Quadi; but he is only known in this passage.

Chapter 43. The reason why the Cotini should be ashamed because they have iron to mine is that they might use it to make weapons and win their freedom, instead of tamely paying tribute.

The gods are two in number, brothers and young men. Their native name is the Alci (probably so, rather than Alces). The 'interpretatio Romana' means the translation as far as possible into Latin—the equation, as near as possible, to gods in the

Roman Pantheon. Castor and Pollux, the Dioscuri, heavenly twins, saviours on land and sea, are the obvious choice.

Some editors declare that the priest 'muliebri ornatu' ('in woman's dress') only had a woman's head-dress, perhaps a long veil. But Anderson adds 'a long robe'. What occasion is there to restrict 'ornatus' to head-gear?

Chapter 45. The Sun-god (Sol) was commonly represented in ancient art as a charioteer, with a crown of rays on his head, stepping into a car, which four horses are about to draw upwards from the waves.

Anderson denies that the language of the Aestii can have been like the British, but can we be so sure? The Anglo-Saxon language swallowed up British, almost without leaving a trace. This is much more intelligible if British was like some German dialects.

Amber seems to have been found from very early times, and there was an 'amber route' from the North Sea to Southern Europe. Apparently there was for some centuries a decline in its use, until a Roman demand sprang up towards the end of the Republic.

Chapter 46. The ugly Sarmatian 'features' mean the gaping nostrils and slanting eyes of the Mongolians.

GLOSSARY OF PERSONS, PLACES AND CERTAIN SUBJECTS

References are to Sections of Introduction, I., and to chapters of Agricola, A., and Germania, G.

ABNOBA. G. 1. The Black Forest.

AEDILE. I. xii.

AEMILIUS SCAURUS, M. A. 1. Consul 115 and 107 B.C.

AESTII. G. 45. On East coast of Baltic, in Esthonia.

AFRICA. I. xiii. A. 42; G. 2. Senatorial province, 146 B.C.

AGRICOLA. *See* JULIUS.

AGRIPPINENSES. G. 28. The people of Cologne (Colonia). founded by Claudius in A.D. 50, with the name of his wife, Agrippina II.

ALA. I. xiv; A. 37. Squadron of cavalry.

ALBAN CITADEL. A. 45. The villa of Domitian on the Alban Mount, the scene of his secret councils.

ALBIS. I. ix; G. 41. The Elbe. Augustus gave up the attempt to advance his frontier to it after the destruction of Varus in A.D. 9.

ALBRINIA (or ALBRUNA). *See* AURINIA.

ALCI. (Alces). G. 43. Brother gods, like Castor and Pollux, worshipped by the Naharvali.

ALPS, RAETIAN. G. 1. Mount St. Gotthard.

AMBER. G. 45.

ANGLII. G. 40. In Schleswig; ancestors of the Angles.

ANGRIVARII. G. 33, 34. On both banks of the Middle Weser.

ANTONINUS PIUS. I. vii. Emperor, A.D. 138–161.

AQUITANIA. A. 9. Imperial province in S. Gaul, *c.* 27 B.C.

ARAVISCI. G. 28. In north-east Hungary.

ARCADES. A. 21. Centres of shopping and gossip.

ARIOVISTUS. I. x.

ARISTOTLE. I. ix. Great Greek philosopher and writer, 384–323 B.C.

ARMINIUS. I. x. Hermann, chief of the Cherusci, victor over Varus in A.D. 9.

ARMS. I. ix. G. 6, 13.

ARMY. I. viii, xiii, xiv.

ARSACES. G. 37. Legendary founder of the Parthian kingdom, 248 B.C. The name was regularly borne by later Parthian kings.

ARULENUS RUSTICUS, L. JUNIUS. A. 2, 45. Sentenced to death *c.* A.D. 93 for his eulogy of Thrasea Paetus.

AS. I. xiv. Roman copper coin, about ½*d*.

ASCIBURGIUM. G. 3. Near Asberg on Lower Rhine.

ASIA. I. i, xii. A. 6, 42; G. 2. Senatorial province, 133 B.C.

ATILIUS RUFUS. A. 40.

ATTICUS, AULUS. A. 37.

AUGUSTUS. I. i, v, x, xi, xiii, xiv; A. 13. First Roman Emperor, 27 B.C.–A.D. 14. *See also* CAESAR.

AURELIUS SCAURUS, M. I. x; G. 37. Consul, 108 B.C., legate of Mallius Maximus, and with him routed by the Cimbri and Teutoni at Arausio (Orange), 105 B.C.

AURINIA. G. 8.

AUSPICES. G. 10.

AUXILIA. I. xiv ; A. 35.

AVIONES. G. 40. In North Frisian islands.

*

BAEBIUS. *See* MASSA.

BANQUETS. I. ix; A. 21; G. 22. A luxurious vice of the Empire.

BARRITUS (or BARDITUS). G. 3. German war-chant.

BASTARNAE. G. 46. Along line of Carpathians, from Galicia southwards.

BATAVI. I. viii; A. 36; G. 29. On Rhine island, between Rhine and Waal.

BATHS. A. 21. A luxurious vice of the Empire.

BIGATI. G. 5. Denarii of the Roman Republic, with a two-horse chariot (*biga*) on the reverse.

BODOTRIA. I. vii; A. 23, 25. The Forth.

BOIHAEMIUM, BOII. I. x; G. 28, 42. Bohemia. The Boii were expelled from it in 8 B.C. by the Marcomanni.

BORESTI. A. 38. Unknown tribe of the Highlands.

BOUDICCA. I. v, xi; A. 16, cp. 31. Queen of the Iceni in East

Anglia. Led revolt against Rome in A.D. 61. Means 'Victory.' 'Boadicea' is an incorrect modern form.

BRIGANTES. I. v, vii; A. 17, 31. North of Trent and Humber, mainly in Yorkshire.

BRITAIN (BRITANNIA, BRITANNI). I. iv ff.; A. *passim;* G. 45. Imperial province, A.D. 43.

BRUCTERI. I. x, G. 33. Near Münster.

BURI. G. 43. In Moravia.

*

CAECILIUS METELLUS, C. G. 37. Consul, 113 B.C.

CAEPIO. *See* SERVILIUS.

CAESAR (=Emperor), I. xii, A. 4.

CAESAR (=Prince), I. xii.

CAESAR (=Augustus), G. 37.

CAESAR. *See* JULIUS and under names of Emperors.

CAESAR, C. (CALIGULA). I. v, x, xi; A. 4, 13, 44; G. 37. Emperor, A.D. 37–41.

CALEDONIA. I. vi; A. 10, 11, 25 ff., 31. The Highlands.

CALGACUS. A. 29 ff.

CALIGULA. *See* CAESAR, C.

CAMULODUNUM (COLCHESTER-COLONY). I. v; A. 14, 16, 31, 32. *See* COLONY.

CARATACUS (CARACTACUS). I. v.

CARBO. *See* PAPIRIUS.

CARUS METTIUS. A. 45. A hated informer under Domitian.

CASSIUS LONGINUS, L. G. 37. Consul 107 B.C., defeated by the Tigurini, allies of the Cimbri.

CASTOR. G. 43. He and Pollux, the Heavenly Twins, were 'Saviour Gods' by land and sea.

CAVALRY. I. xiv; A. 35 ff.; G. 6, 32.

CENTURION. I. xiv; A. 15, 18, 19, 22, 28.

CENTURY. I. xiv.

CEREALIS. *See* PETILLIUS.

CHAMAVI. G. 33, 34. Moved by Nero Drusus into Overyssel in Holland.

CHARIOTEERS (WAR-). A. 35, 36.

CHASUARII. G. 34. North of Osnabrück.

CHATTI. I. x, xi; G. 29, 30–32, 35, 36, 38. In Hesse. Domitian waged war on them in A.D. 83 and 89.

CHAUCI. G. 35, 36. From Lower Ems to Elbe.

CHERUSCI. I. x; G. 36. On Middle Weser. Their chief, Arminius, destroyed Varus and his legions in A.D. 9.

CHIEFS. I. ix; G. 11–15, 22.

CICERO, M. TULLIUS. I. i. Great Roman orator and writer, 1st century B.C.

CIMBRI. I. x; G. 37. In Jutland. Migrated with Teutoni in 113 B.C., won many victories over Rome, harried Gaul and Spain, finally defeated at Vercellae in North Italy, 101 B.C.

CIVICA CEREALIS, C. VETTULENUS. A. 42. Governor of Asia, put to death by Domitian, c. A.D. 90.

CIVILIS. I. x, xi. Leader of revolt of Batavi and Germans against Rome, A.D. 69.

CLAUDIUS. I. v, xi; A. 13. Emperor, A.D. 41–54. Conquered Britain, A.D. 43.

CLOTA. I. vii; A. 23. The Clyde.

CLOTHING. G. 17.

COGIDUMNUS (COGIDUBNUS). A. 14. British king, in Hampshire. Set up a famous inscription at Regnum (Chichester).

COHORS. I. xiv; A. 37.

COLLEGA POMPEIUS, SEX. A., 44. Consul, A.D. 94.

COLONY (COLCHESTER). I. v; A. 14, 16, 31, 32.

COMITIUM. A. 2.

COMPANIONS. G. 13, 14.

CONSECRATION. I. xii.

CONSUL. I. xii; A. 9.

CONSULARS. A. 7, 40, 42.

CONVENTUS (ASSIZES). I. xiii; A. 9.

CORN. I. xiii; A., 19, 31.

CORNELIUS NEPOS. I. iii. Roman writer of biographies, end of first century B.C.

CORNELIUS TACITUS, P. I. i ff.; A. 9, 45, etc.

COTINI. G. 43. On Upper Gran, tributary of the Danube.

CRASSUS. See LICINIUS.

CUNOBELINUS (CYMBELINE). I. v.

*

DACIA. I. ix–xi; A. 41; G. 1. Imperial province, A.D. 106. In A.D. 98 still ruled by a native king, Decebalus.

DANUVIUS. I. x; G. 1, 29, 41, 42. The Danube.

DATES, ROMAN. Kalends were the first of the month, Nones the fifth, Ides the thirteenth (in March, May, July and October Nones were the seventh, Ides the fifteenth). Dates were reckoned backwards from these days.

DECUMATES, AGRI. I. x; G. 29. In modern Hesse, Baden and Wurtemberg.

DENARIUS. G. 5. The standard silver coin of Rome, worth about tenpence. *See also* BIGATI and SERRATI.

DIDIUS GALLUS, A. I. v; A. 14. Governor of Britain, A.D. 52–57.

DIOCESIS. I. xiii.

DIVUS. I. xii. *See also under* EMPERORS.

DOMITIA DECIDIANA, A. 6.

DOMITIAN. I. i, ii, iii, x, xi, xiv; A. 7, 39 ff. Emperor, A.D. 81–96.

DRUSUS. *See* NERO DRUSUS.

DRUSUS, son of TIBERIUS. I. xi.

DRUSUS GERMANICUS. G. 34. The same as Nero Drusus.

DULGUBNII. G. 34. Perhaps on Middle Allier and Leune.

*

ELISII. *See* HELISII.

EMPERORS. I. xi ff.; *and see under* Names.

EUDOSES. G. 40. In South Jutland.

FABIUS RUSTICUS. A. 10. Roman historian, contemporary with Tacitus.

FENNI. G. 46. In Finland.

FLEET. I. xiv; A. 25, 26, 29, 38; G. 44.

FORTS. I. vi, viii; A. 22, 23, 25, 32.

FORUM (FORA). A. 2, 21, 39, 43. A public square. The Roman forum, close to Palatine and Capitol, was the chief centre of Roman public life.

FORUM IULII. A. 4. Fréjus.

FOSI. G. 36. Perhaps north-east of Hanover.

FRAMEA. G. 6, 11, 13. The German spear.

FREEDMEN. I. ix; A. 18, 19, 40–43; G. 25, 44.

FRISII. A. 28; G. 34, 35. In Friesland.

FRONTIER. A., 41; G. 29.

FRONTINUS. *See* JULIUS.

*

GAIUS CAESAR. *See* CAESAR, C.

GALBA. I. xi; A. 6. Emperor, A.D. 68, 69.

GALLIA. I. x; A. 10, 11, 21, 24, 32; G. 1, 2, 5, 27–29, 37, 43. Imperial provinces, *c.* 27 B.C. Belgica, Lugdunensis and Aquitania. A fourth province,

Narbonensis, was older—
senatorial, 121 B.C.

GALLUS. *See* DIDIUS.

GAMBRIVII. G. 2. Perhaps ancestors of the Sugambri, between the Lippe and the Westerwald.

GAMES. A. 6.

GERMANIA (GERMANY). I. ix, x; A. 10, 11, 13, 15, 28, 32, 39, 41; G. *passim*. The Roman 'provinces' of Germany (Upper and Lower) were narrow strips of military occupation on the left bank of the Rhine —Imperial, *c.* A.D. 17.

GERMANICUS. I. x, xi; G. 37. Son of Nero Drusus, adopted son of Tiberius. Campaigned in Germany, A.D. 14–16.

GLAESUM (AMBER). G. 45.

GOTHONES. G. 43. The Goths. East of Lower Vistula. Originally came from South Sweden.

GRAECIA. A. 4; G. 3. Senatorial province (Achaea), 146 B.C.

GRAECINUS. *See* JULIUS.

GRAUPIUS, MONS. I. vi; A. 29 ff. The modern 'Grampians' is a false form.

*

HADRIAN. I. vii, xi. Emperor A.D. 117–138.

HARII. G. 43. In South-East Germany. Perhaps ancestors of the Vandals.

HECATAEUS. I. ix. Early Greek historian, 6th to 5th century B.C.

HELISII. G. 43. In South-East Germany.

HELLUSII. G. 46. Fabulous people in North.

HELVECONES. G. 43. In East Germany.

HELVETII. G. 28. In Switzerland.

HELVIDIUS PRISCUS, THE ELDER. A. 2. Put to death by Vespasian, *c.* A.D. 74.

HELVIDIUS PRISCUS, THE YOUNGER. A. 45. Son of the above. Put to death by Domitian.

HERCULES. G. 3, 9, 34. As god, equals German Thor; as hero, German Siegfried.

HERCYNIUS SALTUS (SILVA). G. 28, 30. Wooded hills from Rhine to Carpathians (the Jura, etc.).

HERENNIUS SENECIO. A. 2, 45.

HERMINONES. G. 2.

HERMUNDURI. G. 41, 42. On Danube and in Franconia and Thuringia.

HERODOTUS. I. ix. Great Greek historian of the Persian Wars, 5th century B.C.

HIBERIA. A. 11. Spain.

HIBERNIA. I. ii, vi; A. 24. Ireland.

HIPPOCRATES. I. ix. Great Greek medical writer, 5th century B.C.

HISPANIA. A. 10, 11, 24; G. 37. Roman provinces: Lusitania and Tarraconensis imperial, Baetica senatorial, after 25 B.C.

HORSES. G. 10.

HUNDRED. I. ix; G. 6, 12.

*

IMPERATOR. I. xii; A. 39.

INGAEVONES. G. 2.

INTIMILIUM. A. 7. Ventimiglia, seventeen miles from Nice.

IRON. G. 6.

ISIS. G. 9. The famous mother-goddess of Egypt.

ISOCRATES. I. iii. Greek orator and essayist, 4th century B.C.

ISTAEVONES. G. 2.

ITALIA. G. 2, 37. Italy.

*

JULIA PROCILLA. A. 4. Mother of Agricola.

JULIUS AGRICOLA, CN. I. i ff., xi, xii; A. passim.

JULIUS, DIVUS. I. ii–v, ix–xi; A. 13, 15; G. 28, 37. Name of Julius Caesar, the Dictator, after death and consecration.

JULIUS FRONTINUS, SEX. I. v, vi; A. 17. Governor of Britain, A.D. 74–77. Wrote on Aqueducts and Stratagems.

JULIUS GRAECINUS. A. 4. Father of Agricola.

JUNIUS MAURICUS RUSTICUS. A. 45. Exiled by Domitian.

*

KINGS. A. 12–15; G. 7, 10, 11, 12, 43, 44.

KNIGHTS. I. xii–xiv; A. 4.

*

LAERTES. G. 3.

LANGOBARDI. G. 40. The Lombards. In North-east Hanover.

LAUREL-WREATHED DESPATCHES. A. 18. Used to announce victory.

LAW, ADMINISTRATION OF. A. 6.

LEGATUS CONSULARIS. I. xiv; A. 7.

LEGATUS LEGIONIS. I. xiv; A. 7.

LEGATUS PRAETORIUS. I. xiv; A. 7.

LEGATUS PROVINCIAE. I. xiii; A. 14 ff.

LEGIO II ADIUTRIX. I. viii.

LEGIO II AUGUSTA. I. viii.

LEGIO VI VICTRIX. I. viii.

LEGIO VIII AUGUSTA. I. viii.

LEGIO IX HISPANA. I. vi, viii;
A. 26, 34.

LEGIO XIV GEMINA MARTIA.
I. viii.

LEGIO XX VALERIA VICTRIX.
I. viii; A. 7.

LEGIONS. I. viii, xiv; A. 35.

LEMOVII. G. 43. In North-
East Germany.

LEVY. A. 7, 13, 15, 31.

LIBURNICA. I. xiv; A. 28. A
swift, light warship.

LICINIUS CRASSUS, M. G. 37.
Defeated and killed by Parthians at Carrhae, 53 B.C.

LIGURIA. A. 7.

LIVIUS, T. I. ix; A. 10. Livy,
great Roman historian of the
age of Augustus.

LOTS. G. 10.

LUGII (LYGII). G. 43. A
large group of South-eastern
Germans.

*

MALLIUS MAXIMUS, CN. G.
37. Consul, 105 B.C., defeated
in that year by Cimbri at
Orange (Arausio).

MANIMI. G. 43. In South-East
Germany.

MANIPLE. I. xiv; A. 28.

MANNUS. G. 2.

MARCOMANNI. I. x; G. 42, 43.
In Bohemia.

MARCUS AURELIUS. I. x.
Emperor, A.D. 161–180.

MARIUS, C. I. x; G. 37. Defeated
Teutoni at Aix-en-Provence
(Aquae Sextiae) in 102 B.C.,
and, with Catulus, defeated the
Cimbri at Vercellae in 101 B.C.

MAROBODUUS. I. x; G. 42.

MARRIAGE, GODS OF. G. 18.

MARS. G. 9. Roman god of
war, the German Tiu.

MARSI. G. 2.

MARSIGNI. G. 43. North or
north-east of Bohemia.

MASSA BAEBIUS. A. 45. Notori-
ous informer under Domitian.
On trial in A.D. 93 for abuses
committed as governor of
Baetica.

MASSILIA. A. 4. Marseilles.
Founded by Greeks in the
7th century B.C.

MATER DEUM. G. 45. German
goddess, Nerthus or Freyga(?),
the Roman Cybele.

MATTIACI. G. 29. On Rhine
and Main. 'Aquae Mattiacae',
the modern Wiesbaden.

MAURICUS RUSTICUS. See
JUNIUS.

MAXIMUS. *See* MALLIUS.

MERCURIUS. G. 9. Equals the German Odin (Wodan).

MESSALINUS, L. VALERIUS CATULUS. A. 45. Blind informer under Domitian.

METALS, PRECIOUS. I. ix; G. 5.

METELLUS. *See* CAECILIUS.

METTIUS. *See* CARUS.

MINES. A. 31, 32.

MOENUS. G. 28. The Main.

MOESIA. A. 41. Bulgaria. Imperial Province, A.D. 6 (?): later, two provinces, 'Upper' and 'Lower', *c.* A.D. 86.

MONA. I. v; A. 14, 18. Anglesey.

MONEY. G. 5.

MUCIANUS, LICINIUS. A. 7. Governor of Syria, A.D. 69, chief supporter of Vespasian in his bid for Empire.

*

NAHARVALI (or NAHANARVALI). G. 43. In Silesia.

NAMES. I., A. and G. *passim*. A Roman commonly had three names: (1) a *praenomen*, personal name, L = Lucius, Sex. = Sextus, etc. (2) a *nomen*, name of his clan (*gens*) —*e.g.*, Flavius, Iulius. (3) A *cognomen*, name of his family —*e.g.*, Caesar, Scaurus. An extra name (*agnomen*) was occasionally added: it might refer to a personal characteristic—*e.g.*, Cicero = 'warty' —or to an honour won—*e.g.*, Germanicus, 'Conqueror over Germany'.

NARISTI. G. 42. West of the Bohemian forest.

NEMETES. G. 28. In region of Speyer.

NERO. I. ii, v, xi; A. 6, 45. Emperor, A.D. 54–68.

NERO (= TIBERIUS). G. 37. An exceptional use.

NERO DRUSUS. I. x; G. 37. Brother of Tiberius. Fought in Germany 12–9 B.C. and died there in the latter year.

NERTHUS. G. 40. Terra Mater or Mother Earth.

NERVA. I. i, iii, x, xi; A. 3. Emperor, A.D. 96–98. In A.D. 97 adopted Trajan.

NERVA TRAJANUS. *See* TRAJANUS.

NERVII. G. 28. Round Bavai and Cambrai.

NORICUM. G. 5. The Tyrol. Imperial province (procuratorial), *c.* 15 B.C.

NUITONES (NUITHONES). G. 40. In Jutland (?).

OCCIDENS. A. 30; G. 45. The West.

OCEANUS. A. 10, 12, 15, 25, 40; G. 1–3, 17, 34, 37, 40, 43, 44.

ORCADES. I. iv; A. 10. The Orkneys.

ORDOVICES. A. 18. In Central and North Wales.

ORIENS. A. 30, 44; G. 37, 45. The East.

ORNAMENTS OF TRIUMPH. A. 40, 44.

OSI. G. 28, 43. Near the river Eipel, on Danube.

OSTORIUS SCAPULA, P. I. v; A. 14. Governor of Britain, A.D. 47–52.

OTHO. I. xi; A. 7. Emperor, A.D. 69.

OXIONES. G. 46. Fabulous people in north.

*

PACORUS. G. 37. Son of Parthian king, Orodes; killed in battle against Ventidius, 38 B.C.

PAETUS. *See* THRASEA.

PALACE. A. 40. On the Palatine Hill in Rome.

PANNONIA. I. x; A. 41; G. 1, 5, 28, 43. Hungary. Imperial province, *c.* A.D. 10.

PAPIRIUS CARBO, CN. G. 37.

Defeated by the Cimbri at Noreia, 113 B.C.

PARTHIA. I. ix, xi; G. 17, 37.

PATRICIANS. A. 9.

PAULINUS. *See* SUETONIUS.

PEARLS. A. 12.

PETILLIUS CEREALIS. I. v, x; A. 8, 17. Governor of Britain, A.D. 71–74.

PETRONIUS TURPILIANUS. I. v; A. 16. Governor of Britain, A.D. 61–63.

PEUCINI (BASTARNAE). G. 46. On island of Danube.

PHILOSOPHERS. A. 2, 4, 46.

PLAUTIUS, AULUS. I. v; A. 14. Governor of Britain, A.D. 44–47.

PLINY THE ELDER. I. iv, ix. Roman official and historian, died A.D. 79.

PLINY THE YOUNGER. I. i. Roman orator and letter-writer, contemporary of Tacitus.

PLUTARCH. I. iii. Great Greek writer of biography, first to second century A.D.

POENI. G. 37. The Carthaginians, famous for their three wars fought against Rome, 264–241, 218–202 and 149–146 B.C.

POLICE. A. 2.

POLLUX. G. 43. He and Castor, the Heavenly Twins, were Saviour gods by land and sea.

POMPONIUS MELA. I. iv. Roman writer on geography, 1st century A.D.

PONTICUM MARE. G. i. The Black Sea.

POSIDONIUS. I. ix. Greek philosopher and historian, *c.* 135–50 B.C.

PRAEFECTUS. A. 22.

PRAEFECTUS ALAE. I. xiv.

PRAEFECTUS CLASSIS. I. xiv; A. 38.

PRAEFECTUS COHORTIS. I. xiv; A. 37.

PRAEFECTUS PRAETORIO. I. xii, xiv.

PRAEFECTUS URBI. I. xii, xiv.

PRAETOR. I. xii; A. 6.

PRAETORIAN GUARD. I. xiv.

PRAETORII. A. 7. Ex-praetors.

PRIESTS. A. 9; G. 7, 10, 11, 40.

PRINCEPS (Emperor) I. xii.

PRISCINUS (or PRISCUS). A. 44. Consul, A.D. 93.

PRISCUS. *See* HELVIDIUS.

PROCILLA. *See* JULIA.

PROCONSUL. I. xiii; A. 6, 42 ff.

PROCURATOR. I. xii, xiii; A. 9, 15.

PROPRAETOR. I. xiii.

PROVINCES. I. xii–xiv.

PUBLICANUS. G. 29. Taxgatherer.

PYTHEAS. I. iv. Of Massilia, traveller and writer, late 3rd century B.C.

*

QUADI. I. x; G. 42, 43. In Moravia.

QUAESTOR. I. xii, xiii; A. 6.

QUINTILIUS VARUS, P. I. x; G. 37. Destroyed with three legions by Arminius in the Teutoburger Wald, A.D. 9.

*

RAETIA. G. 1, 3, 41. East Switzerland. Imperial province (procuratorial), *c.* 15 B.C.

RELIGION. I. xii; G. 7–9, 18, 29, 39, 40, 43, 45.

REUDIGNI. G. 40. In Holstein.

RHAETIA. *See* RAETIA.

RHENUS. I. x; G. 1–3, 28, 29, 32, 34, 41, 45. The Rhine.

ROMANI. A. *passim.* G. 28, 30, 34, 41, 43.

RUFUS. *See* ATILIUS.

RUGII. G. 43. On West of Vistula in Pomerania.

RUSTICUS. *See* ARULENUS and FABIUS.

RUTILIUS RUFUS, P. A. 1. Consul 105 B.C.; unjustly condemned in 92 B.C. for extortion in Asia, he retired into residence there.

*

SALARY OF PROCONSUL. A. 42.

SALLUST. I. i, iii. Roman historian, 1st century B.C.

SALVIUS TITIANUS. A. 6. Proconsul of Asia, A.D. 63–64, brother of Otho, Emperor, A.D. 69.

SAMNITES. G. 37. The Samnites fought bitter wars against Rome, c. 343–290 B.C.

SARMATIA. I. x, xi; G. 1, 17, 43, 46. North of Danube.

SCAPULA. See OSTORIUS.

SCAURUS. See AEMILIUS and AURELIUS.

SCOUTS. A. 26, 38.

SEMNONES. G. 39. Between Middle Elbe and Oder.

SENATE. I. i, xi–xiv; A. 4, 40, 45.

SENECIO. See HERENNIUS.

SEPTIMIUS SEVERUS. I. vii. Emperor, A.D. 193–211.

SERRATI, G. 5. Republican denarii with notched edge.

SERVILIUS CAEPIO, Q. G. 37. Consul 106 B.C., defeated by Cimbri at Orange (Arausio) in 105 B.C.

SHOWS. G. 19, 24.

SILANUS, M. A. 4. Father of first wife of Gaius Caesar: put to death by him in A.D. 38.

SILURES. I. v; A. 11, 17. In South Wales and Monmouthshire.

SITONES. G. 45. Perhaps in Finland.

SLAVES. I. ix; A. 15, 19, 31; G. 20, 24, 25, 38, 40, 45.

SOL. G. 45. The Sun-God.

SQUADRON OF CAVALRY. I. xiv; A. 18, 37.

STRABO. I. iv, ix. Greek writer on geography, late 1st century B.C.

SUARINI (SUARDONES). G. 40. On coast of Mecklenburg (?).

SUCCESSION. I. xii.

SUEBI. I. x; A. 28; G. 2, 9, 38, 39, 41, 43, 45, 46. Generic name for Germans of North and East.

SUETONIUS. I. iii. Roman writer of biography, 1st to 2nd century A.D.

SUETONIUS PAULINUS, C. I. v; A. 5, 14, 16, 18. Governor of Britain, A.D. 59–61.

SUIONES. G. 44, 45. On Baltic.

SYRIA (SURIA). A. 40. Imperial province, 27 B.C. (first established, senatorial 64 B.C.).

*

TACITUS. I. i ff.; A. 9, 45.

TANAUS. A. 22. Tweed or Scottish Tyne (?).

TAXES. I. xiii.

TENCTERI. G. 32, 33, 38. On Middle Rhine to East of Usipi (q.v.).

TERRA MATER. G. 40. Mother Earth. Also called Nerthus.

TEUTOBURGERWALD. I. x.

TEUTONI. I. x.

THRASEA PAETUS. P. A. 2. Famous stoic driven by Nero to suicide in A.D. 66.

THULE (THYLE). A. 10. The Shetlands.

TIBERIUS. I. x, xi, xiv; A. 13. Emperor, A.D. 14–37. *See also* NERO.

TITIANUS. *See* SALVIUS.

TITUS. I. xi. Emperor, A.D. 79–81.

TOGA. A. 9, 21. The national Roman wear for men in peace, a thick woollen garment.

TOGATI. A. 9. Wearers of the toga—Roman civilians.

TRAJANUS, (NERVA). I. i, iii, vii, ix, x, xi; A. 3, 44; G. 37. Emperor, A.D. 98–117.

TREBELLIUS MAXIMUS, M. I. v; A. 16. Governor of Britain, A.D. 63–69.

TREVERI. G. 28. Treves (Trier).

TRIBOCI. G. 28. On Rhine, near Strasbourg.

TRIBUNICIAN POWER. I. xii.

TRIBUNUS MILITUM. I. xiv; A. 5.

TRIBUNUS PLEBIS, I. xii; A. 6.

TRIBUTE. A. 13, 19, 29, 31.

TRIUMPH. A. 39, 40, 44.

TRIUMVIRI (CAPITALES). A. 2. Commissioners of Police.

TRUCCULENSIS PORTUS. A. 38. Unknown harbour, on Firth of Tay (?).

TUDER (TUDRUS). G. 42. Famous king of the Quadi.

TUISTO. G. 2.

TUNGRI. I. viii, x; A. 36; G. 2. On east bank of Lower Rhine: originally called 'Germans'.

TURPILIANUS. *See* PETRONIUS.

*

UBII. G. 28. Settled, as 'Agrippinenses', in Cologne.

ULIXES. G. 3. Ulysses (Homer's Odysseus).

URBAN COHORTS. I. xiv.

USIPI (USIPETES). I. vi, viii; A. 28, 32; G. 32. Between Lower Lippe and Yssel.

*

VANDILICI. G. 2. A general name for East German peoples. The Vandals.

BIBLIOGRAPHY

I give here a very brief selection out of the extensive literature on my subject. My debt is particularly great to Anderson's two volumes. In them, and in the Catalogue of the British Museum Library, fuller information may be found.

AGRICOLA, GERMANIA AND DIALOGUS DE ORATORIBUS

Translation—W. Peterson and M. Hutton (Loeb Classical Library), 1914

W. Hamilton Fyfe. 1908

AGRICOLA AND GERMANIA

Edition—J. H. Sleeman. 1939

AGRICOLA

Edition—J. W. E. Pearce. 1901

S. E. Winbolt. 1913

J. G. C. Anderson (revised edition of H. Furneaux). 1922

Translation (free)—G. J. Acheson. 1938

General—I. A. Richmond. Gnaeus Iulius Agricola. (J.R.S. 1944, pp. 34 ff.)

GERMANIA

Edition—J. G. C. Anderson (revised edition of H. Furneaux). 1938

R. Much. 1937

General—E. Norden. Die germanische Urgeschichte in Tacitus' Germania. 1920